The Trader's Edge

Cashing In On the Winning Strategies of Floor Traders, Commercials & Market Insiders

Grant Noble

PROBUS
PUBLISHING

Chicago, Illinois
Cambridge, England

To my wonderful wife.

*This book would have never been completed
without your patience and love.*

Table of Contents

Introduction

There are three main reasons why I wrote this book:

1. *To tell the truth and nothing but the truth about futures trading.*

   I've written articles for virtually every major futures-oriented publication, but it's become more and more difficult for me to find a publication that will print exactly what I want to say. There's a lot of institution pressure from brokers and vendors not to tell the average futures trader about the mathematics of investing, etc.

2. *To defend a lot of people in our industry (especially floor traders) who get a bum rap from the media and other financial professionals.*

   It's true most people lose money trading futures, but as I will point out in the next chapter, most people don't make money (after inflation, taxes, fees, etc.) in such safe investments as bonds and stocks. The major difference is that in futures (thanks to the low margins), the bad habits of the average investor will just cause him to lose money faster than he would in "safe" investments.

The futures market actually is the fairest market for the average investor. An investor that has mastered his biggest investment problem—emotional, lazy decision making—will find the futures market gives him the best rewards for the least effort of any investment vehicle.

3. *Finally, I want to warn investors about the difficult investing environment that lies directly ahead.*

    Investors who assume the recent bull market in stocks and bonds will continue forever (with only a few small interruptions) are going to lose most of their assets the next few years. Investors who rely on inflation hedges like precious metals and real estate will also be sorely disappointed.

    The only investors that are going to survive the next few years intact are those who can go long and short in a variety of markets with a relatively short investment time horizon time (six months at most). True, there will be other vehicles (like options and other derivatives) that can accomplish many of the same things futures can. But for the average investor, futures will be the investing instrument of choice. I believe this book has techniques that will be new to even experienced and sophisticated futures traders. But it's my fervent hope this book will be the catalyst for thousands of average investors to take off the blinders, investigate the futures market, learn how to trade it, and thus save their assets in the coming economic distress.

To this end, I've tried to write only about inexpensive and easy-to-use trading techniques designed with the average investor in mind. I've also tried to avoid techniques pushed in every magazine and brokerage office. If you want to learn about RSI, Elliott Waves, etc., this is not the book for you. But if you want the trader's edge, the techniques used by the real winners in futures trading (floor traders, commercials, and financial insiders), read on.

Chapter One

Why Every Investor Should Learn How to Trade Futures

Stock and Return on Investment

Stockbrokers like to trot out the fact that common stocks have been the best investment vehicle this century. Supposedly they have generated better total returns (capital appreciation plus dividends) than gold, bonds, or even the average real estate investment.

For the sake of argument, let's assume this fact is true. Let's assume stocks are the best way to go among common investment vehicles. Is this great return on common stocks all it's cracked up to be?

From February 1926 to February 1993 the S&P 500 averaged a 10.4 percent total return (capital gains plus dividends). After subtracting the 3.1 percent CPI inflation rate during this period, that's still a 7.3 percent return. A 7.3 percent real return will double your assets (even after inflation is factored out) in less than 10 years.

At this point the average investor might say, "Why should I worry about finding a successful trading method, especially in the ultrarisky futures market, when 'hold-and-sweat' in the stock market will give me such a good average return?"

In the first place, this return assumes you had enough money to buy all the stocks in the S&P 500. Round lots (100 shares) of just the 30 Dow stocks is a big hunk of change (over $100,000 today at full margin). Index funds (which track a popular average like the S&P 500) are a phenomena of only the last few decades.

If you couldn't buy the entire S&P 500 (or even the Dow) all at once, then you would have had to buy odd lots (less than 100 shares), which would add greatly to your trading costs. Even if you had the unusual psychological stamina to avoid margin buying, ignore stock crashes, ride out many years of below-average yields, and be satisfied with only an average return from boring stock averages, a 7.3 percent return after inflation for hold-and-sweat is still deceptive.

As companies fell in and out of the S&P 500 (or the Dow), you would have to replace them, adding to your initial transaction costs. A 1 percent total for all these costs (commissions and the slippage of buying the asking price and selling the bid price) is very reasonable (especially when you consider the extra cost of odd-lot trading). This would lower your total return from 10.4 percent to 9.4 percent.

Estate taxes and income taxes have been high as 91 percent. About one-third of your 10.4 percent total return is in highly taxed dividends, not capital gains. But let's use the current 28 percent tax on capital gains as a very conservative estimate of taxes. Taxes would further lower your return from 9.4 percent to 6.77 percent. Subtracting the average inflation rate of 3.1 percent would leave you a true return of only 3.67 percent.

Actually, there's many more mice eating your investment cheese. Undoubtedly you invested more at market tops than at market bottoms, even if you were that one in a hundred that avoided selling out at bottoms and doubling up at tops. Your income would naturally fluctuate with the economy (which roughly parallels the stock market).

At market bottoms, you would have less to invest. If you were unemployed or the victim of an emergency (such as an outbreak of war or a natural disaster), you may have had to sell your stocks along with everyone else—right at the bottom. Over time, this could cost you several percent points on your net total return (after taxes and inflation) of 3.67 percent from the S&P 500.

If you add a yearly fee (usually 1 to 2 percent) for a market adviser to administer this strategy (do you think the managers of all those mutual funds you own are working for free?), the most determined hold-and-sweat strategy would probably generate very small, or even negative, returns after taxes, inflation, commissions, financial emergencies, and fees!

In the 202 years of the New York Stock Exchange, we have at least five multiyear periods where owning the average common stock was a losing investment idea after inflation was factored out (1807–1813, 1837–1859, 1907–1921, 1929–1949, 1968–1982). In other words, about 43 percent of the time, stocks have been a long-term bear market where it was difficult if not impossible to make money buying common stocks.

Even during the bullish periods, we have had heart-stopping corrections, crashes, or panics that tried the courage of the most determined investor—the inflation-adjusted correction of 1862–1864, the panics of 1873, 1883, 1893, and 1903; the corrections of 1956–1957 and 1983–1984, and the crashes of 1962 and 1987. How many of you sold all your stocks at the low in 1987?

At this point, I can hear some saying "I have a balanced portfolio of stocks, bonds, and precious metals. I am diversified enough to ride out any investing scenario."

Since 1920, we have had at least seven major periods where none of the usual investment vehicles—stocks, bonds, real estate, precious metals—rose in price (1920–1921, 1929–1932, 1941–1942, 1946–1949, 1968–1970, 1980–1981, 1983–1984). Over the last 75 years, about 15 percent of the time nothing conventional works (later on I will try to show why I feel we are on the verge of another no-win period).

Stocks versus Options

The fact is, any investor who can't go short and take advantage of falling prices is really living in a fool's paradise of diversification. The unlimited risk of short-selling is only a problem for traders that refuse to limit their losses, violate the mathematics of investment (see the next chapter), and would end up a long-term loser any way. It's the futures market's unsurpassed ability to go both long and short that is the main (but not the only reason) why futures are the premier investment vehicle of the mid- to late 1990s.

I once worked with a gentleman I'll call "Sandy," who managed millions of dollars during the great stock bear market of 1973–1974. In a severe bear market, it's very hard to sell a lot of stock on an uptick, as required by stock exchange rules for anyone who isn't a specialist. Sandy described all the maneuvers he had to go through to get off a simple stock short sale. In essence, he had to buy enough stock so he could get an uptick to sell even more stock at a higher price.

During the go-go days of the 1980s, this uptick rule was waived for program traders that sold baskets of stocks against positions in the futures market. During the Crash of 1987, these traders dumped stocks without ceasing. Even sophisticated traders like Sandy could not find an uptick to go short!

This loophole has since been closed, but one fact still stands. It's very difficult for the average stock trader to go short in a bear market. In any market condition, a stock short-seller must keep a balance equivalent to the cost of the stock he is shorting, which is a heavy burden in interest or opportunity costs (unlike the futures market where he earns interest on the money he put up for margin).

Of course, investors can use options (puts) to go short. And the average investor is usually delighted to find out he can only lose what he puts up when he buys an option. Since the majority of options expire worthless, this is often a dubious advantage. I have read statistics that over 90 percent of options lose money from the time they are put on until the time they are offset (or expire worthless). That's even worse than the 80–85 percent losing ratio shown by academic studies of futures traders.

Unlike futures, the option premium (the difference between the price of the option and the underlying security) usually increases with volatility. When a market becomes a bear market, the cost of buying a put option increases. In a bear market in futures, normally you have a negative carry charge market where the futures price is higher than the underlying cash market. You get paid to go short (i.e., if there is no change in the cash price, eventually the futures price will converge with the cash price by going lower).

In any case, any premium (the difference between futures and cash prices, known as *basis*) that exists in futures is only on one side of the trade. If the futures price is below that of cash (as in interest rate futures), this positive carry charge benefits the buyer just as much as it disadvantages the seller (the reverse of the example above). But whether you buy a put or a call, or whether you wish to go long or short a market in options, you will pay a premium on either side of the transaction. You lose either way you go.

Unlike a stock, you don't get dividends (or interest on your margin money as in futures) on an option. Option commissions tend be much higher proportionally than futures. (Discount commissions of $35 are normal on a 100-share option of a security worth $3,000–$5,000. Contrast that with the normal $25 discount commission on a futures contract, which can control up to $250,000 in equivalent cash assets.)

Perhaps the only advantage of options over futures is the ability to make money if there is no change in the market. Professionals often put on strangles (simultaneous selling of an out-of-the-money call and put) and collect the premium on both sides if the underlying market doesn't make a major move. (The majority of time markets are in easily defined trading range markets.)

But even this option advantage is better used with options on futures rather than options on individual stocks. The dirty little secret of the stock market is that it is far more volatile and far less predictable than soybeans, cattle, copper, and other traditional futures contracts.

There are many academic studies that prove this fact, but you really don't need to be an academic to figure this out. Individual stocks that double in price or lose 50 percent of their value in a day are a relatively common occurrence. This type of action is a once-in-a-lifetime occurrence in futures (I can't think of a single example off the top of my head).

In October 1987, the S&P 500 future lost 45 percent of its value in 13 days of trading. The most spectacular commodity crashes—soybeans in June 1973, cattle in August 1973, sugar in November 1974, silver in January 1980, and crude oil in January 1986—all took about three times as long to travel the same distance (a 45 percent collapse).

The reputation for volatility in futures is strictly a function of its low margin requirements. A 5 percent move in a stock from 20 to 21 would only draw a yawn. A 5 percent move in corn (from $2.00 to $2.10 a bushel) is a $500 move approximately equal to the usual margin on corn.

Not only is the stock market more volatile, it's volatility is less predictable than futures. Mergers (or the sudden failure of a merger), preliminary earnings reports, the comments of corporate officials and politicians—all these bolts from the blue can cause a stock to double or lose half its value. Totally unexpected events in futures (like the Russian coup, Chernobyl, etc.) are far more rare and, in any case, hardly ever have the same impact of stock shocks.

A freeze in Brazil can cause coffee prices to triple, but we know that will only occur in the summertime. An orange juice freeze or soybean drought can cause prices to explode, but these events can only come at regular intervals, which can be easily anticipated.

Even regular reports are not so regular in the stock market. Earnings reports can be shifted around in an unexpected manner. Highly touted announcements or press conferences can mysteriously disappear or be rescheduled. Over the last decade, we have seen key reports shift around with the latest investment fad.

In the 1960s, it was earnings. In the 1970s, it was the money supply. In the 1980s, it was the trade deficit. In the 1990s, it's the unemployment report. I don't know what the next critical government report will be in the next decade, but I do know the Pig Crop Report, the USDA crop conditions as of July 1, etc., will basically have the same influence over futures prices tomorrow as they do now. If you are going to use options, it makes sense to use them in the (relatively) regular world of futures rather than the wacky world of individual stocks.

There is a slight tax advantage (thanks to the latest Clinton tax increase) in holding cash assets (such as stocks and precious metals) for a capital gain, which you can't do in futures or other derivatives like options. But capital gains tax breaks can be taken away at any time (as they were in the 1986 tax "reform"). And in order to take advantage of a lower capital gains rate, you need a bull market—which as we've seen only occurs about half the time in stocks. Many investors have seen a winning investment turn into a loser while waiting for the proper time to take a capital gain.

Virtually every investment vehicle outside of futures depends on a market maker or specialist. A market maker or specialist has tremendous advantages over those media demons, futures floor traders, who supposedly make sure no investor can possibly win trading futures.

A market maker can declare an order imbalance and simply shut down trading in an option or a stock. No single pit trader can do that to a future. A floor trader only knows the bid/asks he sees in open outcry in the pit. An order filler may have 1,000 contracts to sell, but he doesn't have to show them all by open outcry in the pit. He can sell them off 50 or 100 contracts at a time until he has sold them all.

By contrast, anyone who wants to sell stock at a specified price must register his order in the specialist's book. In other words, unless a stock trader wants to play "hot potato" by constantly juggling his order size, he gives up any chance of keeping his order size a secret.

As Sandy explained it to me, the specialist (or his friends) are not above stepping in front of a large order by selling a tick or two below this large order. This is supposed to be against the rules; however, wherever you have insider monopolies (rather than the free market of an open outcry auction), you are going to have these eternal problems of human nature.

Did you know that no futures trader has ever lost money due to the failure of a clearing member of the Board of Trade or the Chicago Mercantile Exchange? The New York Stock Exchange can't say that—which is why there is now stock insurance to protect against bankruptcy in stock firms. The clearing system of futures is inherently safer than the system in place for stocks.

Much has been made of the zero sum game of futures, i.e, for every short there is a long, for every winner there is an equal and opposite loser. (Often the loser is a perfectly content hedger who has already locked up a profitable price.) However, this zero sum game aspect of futures has an unexpected bonus in a financial crisis.

Let's use the latest shock in futures as an example. Over the weekend of June 28–29, 1994, a freeze struck Brazil's coffee fields. Coffee opened almost 40 cents higher on Monday's opening from Friday's close—a price move of over 30 percent, or $15,000 per futures contract.

Since the minimum margin for one coffee contract was around $3,000 at the time, it would appear the clearing firm guaranteeing this trade and hundreds of others might be in trouble if the losers reneged and refused to post extra margin or pay their losses. But even if we assume there was no extra money in the losers' accounts (very unlikely) and they refused to send any more money to cover their losses (another unlikely event), the clearing firm is still far from getting into trouble.

Say the clearing firm has a total of 250 short coffee contracts and 200 long coffee contracts on its books before the freeze, or net short 50 contracts. Fifty times $15,000 is $750,000, which is far less than the $1.25 million (450 × $3,000) it has on account for customer margin.

You can see it is very difficult for a futures clearing firm that is clearing accounts from a wide variety of customers to go broke. Only gross overspeculation by its principals could cause such a problem.

(If a clearing firm's owners were net short hundreds of contracts of coffee before the freeze, and if that position represented the overwhelming majority of their assets, then conceivably that clearing firm could go broke. In that case, the commodity clearing corporation of that exchange would guarantee the trades and seize whatever assets the firm and its principals had left. All customer positions and money then would be transferred to solvent clearing firms. This has happened only once in Chicago during the two decades of my experience.)

By contrast, even a "prudent" stock firm could go broke in a meltdown similar to the 1987 crash. A stock investor only has to put up 50 percent margin to purchase a stock, 35 percent to maintain that position. A 45 percent collapse in two weeks (like that which occurred in 1987) could bring a client's balance to negative territory. If that firm's investors were speculating in bonds and other securities that can be purchased for 10 percent margin or less, it could be only a matter of hours before they are in the firm's pocket, so to speak.

The billions in losses racked up banks and brokerage house during the bear market in bonds in 1994 is just the tip of the iceberg of what could happen in a crisis. Through October 1994, the bond market had dropped 15 percent for the year. In a crisis atmosphere, where bonds could go down 50 percent in a few months, there could be trillions in losses.

Yes, stock options are cleared basically the same way as futures in that both the seller and buyer of the option (and their respective clearing firms) guarantee that trade. But the clearing of stock options is far more concentrated in a handful of firms than is futures. It's far more likely the whole stock option clearing system will fail in a 1987-type meltdown than hundreds of clearing firms, which specialize in clearing futures as unconnected as cattle and bonds.

Finally, the futures clearing corporations (to which all futures clearing firms belong) have been in existence for up to 150 years (versus the 20+ years of the option clearing corporations). They have had a far longer time to accumulate assets (through clearing fees charged on every futures trade). These assets are far in excess of the miniscule amount of assets that backs the insurance that "guarantees" stock trading.

As Will Rogers used to say, "I am more concerned about the return of my money than the return on my money." In terms of a potential financial crisis, I think we can safely say the federal government is more likely to renege on its debt than the clearing corporations of the futures market fail to make good on transferring money from futures losers to futures winners.

For smaller investors, the low cost of entry and the ease of true diversification may be a great advantage. For $10,000, you can have a balanced portfolio among the six trillion-dollar markets—metals, currencies, interest rates, agriculturals, crude complex, and stocks (through options on index stock futures), while $10,000 won't buy you even a round lot (100 shares) of a Dow stock like Caterpillar at today's prices.

The price of individual stocks are far more correlated than the futures prices, i.e., the price of IBM, GM, and Disney are far more likely to rise and fall together than the price of cattle, silver, and T-bonds. Even the price of gold stocks are far more tied to the rise and fall of the overall valuation of the stock market than the rise and fall of the Consumer Price Index!

True, to achieve diversification among the six trillion-dollar markets with a $10,000 futures account you may have to control the futures equivalent of $150,000 in cash assets. But because of the negative correlation of futures markets, plus less volatility and chance of negative surprises, the real risk may not be all that much greater than an equivalent amount of margined stocks ... and you don't have to put up $75,000 (50 percent)!

From every rational perspective, the futures market is a better deal, especially for small investors. As I have stated before, all the low margins of the futures market do is speed up the losing investment process of the average investor. The next chapter will discuss the real reasons why 85 percent of futures traders lose. They are the same reasons why 85 percent of stock investors underperform the market averages (which, as we have seen, barely keep up with inflation after expenses and taxes).

Chapter Two

Your Greatest Enemy to Successful Investment

The following is a reprint of an old article I wrote called "The Great Con Game." This article was written specifically for futures but its principles apply to every field of investing. There is no magic formula in any market that can turn you into an instant millionaire. If you are determined to believe that, nothing I say is going to help you.

$$* \; * \; *$$

The Great Con Game[1]

"I was a commodity loser until I discovered I couldn't believe my results..." "To pay my costs, only a select few..." "There will be no second chance, so send money fast..."

If you wonder about these "perfect systems," consider the law of compound interest. Recently, a system advertised a

---

1 Grant Noble, "The Great Con Game," *Futures* (Nov. 1985), Copyright 1985 by Commodities Magazine, Inc., 218 Parkade, Cedar Falls, IA 50613)

2,100 percent return in two years or double your money in five-and-a-half months. Assume it works and its inventor sells 200 of these systems for $1,000 each. Also assume each buyer invests $10,000. With the inventor's $200,000, that's $2.2 million total equity.

After five-and-a-half months, every account has doubled. Then greed takes over. Old investors get 10 new ones, some as "fund managers." Others use copiers. In less than a year, the system has $50 million total equity—a sum impossible to invest without market distortions.

In short, anyone bright enough to invent a system that performs in every market and time period would never jeopardize it by selling it to the public. He can make far more by trading it for himself and his clients.

"Holy Grail" Bound

Most traders realize you can't buy a perfect system, but they still believe it exists. There are three main sources of this myth: (1) returns from simple trend-following methods, (2) track records, and (3) experts promoting the latest technical fad.

When I worked for a Midwest stock firm, an Eastern computer expert impressed the bigwigs with his real-time record. A few calculations showed a simple trend-following method would have returned more over the same period. Another source of the perfect system myth is the spectacular but brief track record. A famous technical trader wrote how he made a million. Unfortunately, he went into a losing period soon afterward. Had he continued to sustain the returns shown in his book, it's unlikely he would still he giving seminars.

Consider these system cliches:

✳ "The trend is your friend." Nine of 10 commodities are not trending at any given time. When they breakout, simple trend-following methods will catch it as well as most systems.

* "Risk a dollar to make four." Contrary to what you read, most traders have the discipline to follow their system. Unfortunately, because most commodities are trendless, the four-dollar profit simply is not there. Many system traders are risking a dollar to make 50 cents (after fees, commissions, etc.).

* "Don't put all your eggs into one basket." Why are there more rich scalpers and pyramiders than system traders? Because it's easier to spot a big move if you concentrate on a few markets. Because nine of ten commodities are trendless, a system trader must diversify to ride out the long time between winners.

* "The close is *the* number." Most price movement occurs within an hour of the opening. Long before the computer funds mangle the close to "catch the trend," smart traders are well-positioned for the next day.

* "It's all in the numbers." There are 27 major commodities, at least a dozen major trading methods, several indicators per method, and at least three signals per indicator (long, short, or neutral). To expect any system to handle all these is like asking a computer to write a Mozart symphony.

In the end, nothing can take the place of a trader analyzing and combining all the data into his own winning pattern. For most of us, this takes years of hard work and sometimes unprofitable trading.

No wonder the "perfect system" con game flourishes! The public in its lazy greed wants a quick way to a million. And it can always find "experts" to sell it what it wants.

✳ ✳ ✳

I honestly believe futures trading is the best opportunity for the average investor, and the techniques I will describe later on are some of the best you can use in trading futures. But it is still true: Nothing can take the place of a trader analyzing and combining all the data into his own winning pattern. You can attempt to apply every concept written in this book and still lose.

Why? Because the biggest trading problem you face is not high commissions, lousy fills, insider trading, lack of information, bad advice from your broker, discovering the secret of the (trading) universe, or finding the next Warren Buffet. It's you. Y, O, U, YOU! Your emotions, hidden psychological problems, and preconceived notions are your greatest enemies whether you trade stocks, bonds, options, futures, real estate, precious metals, or what have you.

As Richard Dennis, one of the foremost trading legends of our time, put it: "I always say that you could publish (my) trading rules in the newspaper and no would follow them. The key is consistency and discipline. Almost anybody can make up a list of rules that are 80 percent as good as what (I) taught."[2]

I was a futures broker for six years. Since then I've talked with dozens of investment professionals. Not one of them mentioned a client coming to them and saying, after long study, "I believe these trading principles are the key to success and I want you to help me use them in your area of expertise." Instead, investors always seem to fall into the following four basic categories.

What's Hot or Who's Hot?

This type thinks a specific area (stocks, bonds, futures, real estate, precious metals, etc.) or a specific adviser/broker is his ticket to success. He is another victim of what I call track recorditis.

Suppose I told you the absolutely true, verifiable fact that I made over 500 percent in a two-week period trading futures. Sounds impressive, doesn't it?

But this fact doesn't tell you how I made this 500 percent. It was during the October 1987 stock crash, a time of unprecedented volatility. I stumbled into the profitable side of copper in the beginning and afterwards was able to take advantage of the obvious distortions the stock crash generated in all the other futures markets. As I look back on it now, I really didn't know

---

2 Jack Schwager, *Market Wizards* (New York: Simon & Schuster, 1989), 86.

what I was doing, and I was very blessed not to be 500 percent in the hole instead.

Virtually all the stockbrokers working today have never experienced a major bear market like that of 1973–74. What are they going to recommend if we repeat the 1973–74 experience? The vast majority of mutual funds weren't around 20 years ago. What good will all those great track records be in a 1974 type of environment?

Even if a fabulous track record is not fraudulent, the result of chance, or a massive, once-in-a-generation trend, there are at least two other factors that can make it irrelevant.

First of all, every investment vehicle has dull times when no strategy can make money. If you (or your expert) do not understand this and concentrate only in one area of expertise, you could be very disappointed. More trading fortunes have been built on soybeans than any other commodity I know. Yet in 1985 and 1986, soybean prices moved so little traders were leaving the soybean pits in frustration.

Secondly, even the best traders or advisers choke when given too much money. As assets grow arithmetically, the accompanying psychological and asset allocation problems grow geometrically. Many trading geniuses like Arthur Cutten and Jesse Livermore made millions only to lose at the end. Success went to their heads and they began to disregard the very rules that made them a success in the first place. Like most beginning investors, they began to believe it was their great genius, not their great discipline, that made them winners. Anyone who relies solely on track records to make his investment decisions is bound to be disappointed in the end.

I've Found (Invented) This Surefire System

The finest minds in the country are not the heads of government or big corporations. They are not even on university campuses. The best brains in the world are trying to figure out where stocks, bonds, gold, etc., are going to be tomorrow morning.

My friend Neal Weintraub runs the "Tricks of the Trader" futures trading seminars in Chicago. Everyone who attends has to go through the libraries of the Board of Trade and the Mercantile Exchange. Neil loves to point out that virtually every book, system, newsletter, or seminar published about futures trading ends up on these shelves long before the public knows about them. Even those methods "restricted to the first hundred who pay" get passed around exchanges very quickly, thanks to our local copy machines.

Maybe you are that one in a million that has found something truly original in investing. However, like the Chinese who invented gun powder but didn't know how to use it, you can still lose in the stressful world of trading. It's better to master the simple laws of trading first and find that breakthrough later.

I'm on the Ground Floor of a Great Idea

Of all the things that seduce the average investor, concept investing is the worst. Yes, I know Peter Lynch says that you have a better chance than he does of finding the next Xerox or Wal-Mart. That may be true, but it is also true that Peter has a much better chance of *benefiting* from the next Xerox or Wal-Mart.

Let's say you find a company, commodity, option, etc., that doubles your investment in a short time. If you are the typical investor, you will do one of two things. You will sell your entire position and brag about the profits at the country club. Or you will put most of your life savings in it.

Inevitably, your next Xerox has a small fall in price. Because you've invested most of your money at higher prices, this fall causes you to lose money, panic, and sell just before the next big rise. In either case, you aren't really going to cash in on the next Xerox.

A Peter Lynch will start tracking your hot company as soon as it becomes public. He may miss the initial surge, but his capital and trading techniques will take advantage of the rest of the move.

Or take the "gold bugs." They were absolutely right in condemning paper money and predicting higher precious metal prices in the 1970s. But how many actually took advantage of the big moves? How many threw away what little profits they made by buying high-priced metals in the early 1980s? It's been my experience that only one gold bug in a hundred has made a better than average return over the last twenty years.

Creativity or intelligence has no more to do with successful trading than it does with a successful business. Both need sufficient capital, a well-thought-out plan of operation, and, most of all, the humility to copy those who were successful before you.

True, the greatest traders, like the greatest businessmen, also have creativity and intelligence to go along with elementary trading techniques. But like their business counterparts, often they had to unlearn all they knew before they could really start to succeed. Only when market humiliations forced them to follow the "simple" laws of investing could they begin to use their great talents in the markets.

That's why the ranks of great traders are filled with many college dropouts and very few Ph.D.'s. That's why, like most new businesses, most new investors fail. Their investments fail to keep up with market averages or even inflation. Their returns never justify their opportunity costs in time and treasure. Sadly, the record of new investors is even more dismal than new businesses due to this next and last type of investor.

Where's the Action?

Few start a business to satisfy an urge for excitement and risk. Unfortunately, a casino mentality controls a large segment of investors. As lottery fever grips our society, more and more investors are looking for that easy way to millions. Often they keep playing the market until the money runs out.

This craving for action infects even professionals. Many can't take a vacation without keeping a quote machine and a phone by their side. Many continue to trade even when the shrinking bottom line is screaming, "Stop! Take time out." For every trader who had the courage to quit the business when he lost his touch, there are a dozen other megatraders that continued to trade themselves into oblivion.

Ninety-nine percent of investors that walk into a broker's office fall into one of these four categories. Even the most honest, skilled, and persuasive broker is going to have a hard time convincing these investors to change their losing ways. That takes time, time the average investor doesn't have because of the Mathematics of Investing.

Mathematics of Investing

What do you get when you initiate a trade in stocks, bonds, futures, options, precious metals, or any other investment? An instant loss!

Everyone understands commissions, but not every understands the bid/ask spread. Any trader who isn't a specialist or a pit trader is always going to pay a premium to get in and a premium to get out. He pays the asking price to buy and the bid price to sell.

Let's say our trader is trading S&P 500 futures. Presently the asking price is 450.10 while the bid price is 450.05. If he goes to buy this future, he will pay 450.10. If he goes to sell the future, he will get 450.05. Even if the S&P 500 market remains absolutely the same, our trader will be forced to lose not only his commission but the difference between 450.10 and 450.05 or $25 per contract plus commission.

In our example, we assumed the bid/ask spread was only a minimum fluctuation, or one tick. In the real trading world of stop-loss selling, fast markets, and wild openings and closes, the bid/ask is often more than one tick even in the most liquid markets. Let's say the average bid/ask spread is two ticks, or $50 in the S&P 500 futures market. Let's further assume commissions of $25 for a completed buy and sell. If a trader daytrades just one S&P 500 futures contract each day, that would be about $18,000 ($75 × 240 days) a year in trading expenses (commission plus bid/ask slippage) before any winnings are collected.

If you add in the $750 a month the average trader spends for computerized, real-time futures quotes and other information, you can see why someone with the average $10,000 daytrading account must nearly quadruple his initial investment just to cover trading expenses.

But let's assume that this slippage factor of bid/ask trading plus commissions has been taken care of in our tale of Humble Harry versus Trader Tom.

Humble Harry versus Trader Tom

Trader Tom has developed his own ultrasophisticated, personalized system that makes an honest-to-God 200 percent a year trading futures. Tom spends all his time trading. His normal living expenses are $3,000 a month plus another $1,000 a month to pay for real-time quotes, software, computer depreciation, books, seminars, etc.

Humble Harry uses a simple moving average system that makes 40 percent a year. Harry looks at yesterday's futures prices and puts his orders in at the beginning of the trading day. Harry doesn't need to look at a quote screen all day, so he works another job that pays him $4,000 a month, of which $3,000 goes toward his expenses with the final $1,000 plowed back each month into his trading account. Both Harry and Tom start with a $100,000 trading account.

Harry gets a 2 percent gain the first month, a 1 percent loss the second month followed by monthly gains of 3 percent, 0 percent, 4 percent, 5 percent, 6 percent, 4 percent, 4 percent, 3 percent, 4 percent and .4 percent for an average return of 40 percent. Tom's monthly totals are −20 percent, −10 percent, 0, 0, 20 percent, 20 percent, 20 percent, −10 percent, 0, 30 percent, 40 percent, 47 percent or a 200 percent yearly return. Because Tom trades all the time, he goes for the lowest commission rate and therefore doesn't get T-bill interest on his account balances.

Harry gets the float of .5 percent a month on his account.

At year's end, Harry's account has $162,356.40 while Trader Tom has only $160,094.45. Tom is on his way to ulcers while Harry sleeps like a baby every night.

Sure, I stacked the deck a little bit. I had Tom's winnings come late in the year after expenses and losses had eaten away his equity down to $56,400 in the fourth month of trading. And Harry's 40 percent using a simple moving average may be a trifle above average. But on the whole, these figures are in the ball park.

In real life, the average Tom wouldn't have gone on with his system after his big losses in the second and third month of his trading. The Psychological Law of 10/20 Percent would have taken over.

The Psychological Law of 10/20 Percent

Whenever anything (except normal living expenses) takes more than 10 percent of our income or savings, we become annoyed. This law of humanity is as old as the tithe or the agent's 10 percent. When this expense or loss reaches over 20 percent of our income or savings, we become irate and spend most of our spare time figuring out how to avoid this expense or loss.

That's why the totally oppressed Egyptian peasant and Medieval serf rarely paid more than 20 percent of their income to their landlords.

Societies forced to pay more than 20 percent of their income in taxes, which doesn't come back in the form of some government entitlement, inevitably have tax revolts, go into economic collapse, or are forced to tolerate a huge underground economy that effectively lowers the tax rate.

It's no accident that the percent of federal taxes paid by the average American has been stable at 19 percent of income for the past three decades. The total U.S. tax rate from all sources (state, federal, municipal) is around 42 percent, but when you add in unfunded mandates plus the cost of filling out forms (like the 1040) and the deficit, the real rate is closer to 50 percent.

But direct disbursements (like entitlements, subsidies, etc.) brings that figure down to 20 percent. Politicians instinctively know that this is all they can get away with (at least until recently). In Italy, high tax rates have created an underground economy almost equal to the official economy.

My most vivid lesson in the 10/20 rule was managing money. I started with a $10,000 account and tripled it to $30,000. I took a management fee of 25 percent of the profits, sent my client's original $10,000 home, and started to trade again with the remaining $15,000.

Unfortunately, the account then fell 33 percent to $10,000. My client withdrew all his money to trade it for himself. It didn't matter he was still 100 percent ahead. I had taken a loss greater than 20 percent and so he lost confidence. (He later lost what was left trading the account himself).

Let's say a trading system is right 60 percent of the time (a very good average in the real world). In a perfectly random world, the chances of this system losing 10 trades in a row would be one in a thousand. But trading is not random, and trading systems (and traders) can blow hot and cold for extended periods of time.

If 25 percent of the time the system was right 90 percent, 50 percent of the time it was right 60 percent, and 25 percent of the time it was right 30 percent, that would average out to 60 percent for a given time period. But during the 30 percent correct period, there would a 2.83 percent chance of losing 10 in a row. If this 30 percent period is extended over 250 trades in a three-month period, the odds are 50/50 this system will see 10 losing trades in a row, despite its yearly average of a 60 percent winning ratio.

If you are risking 1 percent of your trading equity on each trade, 10 losses in a row isn't likely to shatter your confidence in a normally successful system. But if you are risking 3 percent of your equity on each trade, the resulting 27 percent loss after 10 losing trades could cause you to abandon the system or stop trading all together.

Now let's go back to our S&P 500 daytrader with $10,000. Let's say his system is right on average 60 percent, but with the fluctuating winning percentages described above. This system wins $300 and loses $125 on an average trade. However, slippage due to commissions and the bid/ask spread causes an extra $75 loss on both ends, raising the average loss to $200 and cutting the average winner to $225. Our one-trade-per-day daytrader makes only a few thousand more than his $9,000-a-year overhead ($750 a month for quotes, seminars, newsletters, etc.).

If this daytrader began to trade three times a day instead of once, theoretically he would make another $23,400 a year if his system continued to perform at 60 percent. But what if he increases trading just when the system is entering the 30 percent winning mode? Over a four-month period of 250 trades, he has a 50/50 chance of losing 10 times in a row and taking a $2,000 loss on a $10,000 starting account. This will probably cause our trader to abandon his system just when it is ready for big gains.

In actuality, it's a very rare futures speculator who doesn't risk more than 1 percent of his equity on a trade. When I was a broker, risking $500, a $1,000, or even $2,000 on a $10,000 account was routine for many of my customers.

The average investor violates the 10/20 percent factor all the time. He routinely puts more than 20 percent of his equity in one stock, one futures contract, etc. With most of his eggs in very few baskets, he becomes liable to jettison any trading plan and trade very emotionally.

These investors begin to track that particular future or stock tick for tick, becoming totally mesmerized. They refuse to take profits ("Just a little more and I'm a millionaire") or losses ("It'll come back") at the appropriate time. These overcommitted investors become oblivious to their danger or to investment opportunities elsewhere.

However, there is another psychological law that probably causes even more investment losses than the 10/20 Percent Law. I call it the 3/21-Day Memory Law.

The 3/21-Day Memory Law

Scientific studies have shown that humans lose about 80 percent of what they learned within three days of having first learned it. Afterwards this memory loss continues gradually until about the 21st day where it stabilizes at about 3 percent permanent memory.

This 3/21-Day Memory Law has many implications for investment strategies, which I will discuss in later chapters. But by far the biggest implication of the 3/21-Day Memory Law is a psychological one.

Ask any professional trader what is his toughest day was and he'll say, "The day after the market has beaten my brains in." The painful memory of one bad trading day can cause market paralysis or erratic trading for up to three weeks. Unless you are thoroughly convinced of the validity of your trading methods, you will be sorely tempted to drop out of trading or at least "modify" your methods to "prevent further losses."

On the other hand, the worst trading I ever saw as a broker was after a spectacular winning day by a client. As a broker, I felt the best thing for the average client was to take a few (small) losses in the beginning to gain humility and respect toward the markets. Novice traders that won in the beginning went out of control in the end, sometimes losing more than their initial investment.

Floor traders or specialists who trade on the exchange floor have many advantages over public traders: a bigger capital base, a far lower cost of market entry, the ability to see the entire flow of orders, etc. But I honestly believe their greatest advantage is that their trading style rarely runs afoul of the 3/21-Day Memory Law.

Trading hundreds of times in a three-day period on the exchange, floor traders may experience a spectacular winning period, but it's very likely they will also experience a losing period that will splash cold water on their "I'm-a-trading-genius-that-can-do-no-wrong" fantasies. Losing periods, on the other hand, rarely extend for more than one day.

Over a 21-day period, a floor trader or exchange specialist

will make enough trades to experience (at least on a small scale) virtually every trading outcome known. Even during years of low volatility or traditional seasonal slowdowns (like holiday periods), he is never bored for weeks on end. The average public trader is very tempted during these slow times to overtrade because every few days, he needs to feel the jolt, the excitement of trading the markets. With a $45 loss built into every trade, that's a proscription for disaster.

Fear (after losing), greed (after winning), boredom (leading to no-chance trading), and ignorance (of the mathematics and psychology of trading) are the Four Horsemen of the Apocalypse for traders. Unless you conquer them, nothing in this book is going to help you make money.

Finding a Guru: No Investing Panacea

What about those hot shot market advisers you read about? Is it possible to find someone who could manage your money and consistently beat the market averages in stocks and beat a simple moving average system in futures (after expenses)? Yes, but it's not very likely.

1. You have to find this adviser before the rest of the world finds out about him and makes it impossible for him to sustain those big returns (especially after those hefty fees). There's also a very real chance he could crack under the strain of managing megamillions.

2. You must avoid "track recorditis" and find someone that can really deliver a superior performance over time in all sorts of markets. An adviser who can only generate above-average returns in a bull market is positively dangerous.

In any case, the more you know how to trade, the better you can separate the wheat from the chaff among outside money managers.

Your Psychological Profile: Can You Stand the Dull World of Winning Futures Trading?

If you trade 100 times a year and it costs (on average) a minimum of $45 to enter the futures market on any one trade, you will have to generate $4,500 a year in trading profits (by correctly guessing the direction of the market) just to break even. That's a 45 percent return on a $10,000 futures account! That brings me to Dull-but-Successful Trading Rule #1:

1. *Never spend more on trading expense and overhead than your futures account will take in T-bill interest.*

    A $100,000 futures account opened today will generate about $4,000 in interest (assuming the standard payout rate of 90 percent of today's T-bill interest of around 4.5 percent). If you spend $100 a month on quotes and research, that leaves you $2,800 or about five trades a month (60 × $45) for trading expenses.

    Five trades a month from a $100,000 account would drive the average futures broker up a wall in frustration. The system gurus who claim returns of 100–200 percent a year would sneer. But here's why the average investor in futures must follow this rule as closely as possible.

    If your total trading expenses (commission, bid/ask slippage, overhead) is going to exceed your guaranteed interest income, you make it far more likely that you will suffer a drawdown during trading that will exceed 10 percent or even 20 percent of a period's starting equity. Unless you've experienced the strain of this type of drawdown, you will never understand the enormous temptation to make emotional decisions (by overtrading or withdrawing into a shell) that ruin trading performance.

    It's this type of irrational, emotional trading that caused the search for the Holy Grail—a mechanical system that never suffers emotional lapses. But now that everyone has a personal computer, which can go through umpteen numerical manipulations of the Sacred Six (High, Low, Open, Close, Volume, and Open Interest), purely mechanical trading is losing its punch. More and more we are seeing false technical breakouts that never follow through to the downside or upside. There is no fundamental reason behind these price movements, only the hum of thousands of computers making the same dumb decisions at the same time.

If you want a better-than-average return in any investment, you are going to have to do something besides what the average investor is doing. Increasingly, even in stocks, the average investor is looking at momentum indicators (like stochastics) and charts to make his decisions.

The techniques described later in this book are not rehashes of the same old technical methods that dominate the investment market. They do offer you the opportunity of making above-average returns, but unfortunately you will have to use your brain as well as your computer. If the human brain is in the equation, you must at all costs keep out the emotional factors that ruins trading decisions. One of those factors is large losses, another is the sheer stress that making many trading decisions in a short period puts on one's brain.

Dull-but-successful Trading Rule #2 is similar to the first rule:

2. *Never risk more than 1 percent (trading risk plus commissions) on any one trade.*

    That means a $5,000 account should only risk $50 a trade, including the cost of commissions. If that means trading only agricultural contracts on the MidAmerica Exchange or out-of-the-money options, so be it.

    We've talked about the psychological problem of losing more than 10 percent or 20 percent. But there are two other mathematical reasons to limit your losses to the smallest ratio possible.

    All trading activity is a struggle to try every investment idea that looks promising in the hopes that one of them will work. The more you lose the less you have to try another trade, another trading method, another investment vehicle. To illustrate this we'll bring back Humble Harry and Trader Tom.

Trader Tom and Humble Harry both start with $100,000. Both lose five trades in a row. Harry keeps his losses to 1 percent of equity—he ends up with $95,100. Tom risks $5,000 a trade and goes down to $75,000. To get to $150,000, Tom must make 100 percent. To get to $150,000, Harry only has to make 57 percent. Tom must outperform Harry by 75 percent to get to the same goal!

Harry is long one contract of coffee before the late June freeze because the moving averages turned bullish a long time ago. Tom is long two contracts because his system takes big risks. Harry makes $15,000, and Tom makes $30,000 over one weekend. Harry is still ahead by $5,000 despite the ulcer-producing risks Tom takes. That brings me to Dull-but-Successful Trading Rule #3:

3. *No matter how intellectually stimulating or exciting to trade, any trading method that, **after expenses**, couldn't beat a simple 18-day moving average system over the same period has to be dropped.*

Charles LeBeau (who edits the *Technical Trader Bulletin* out of Torrance, California) once made a statement something like this at a seminar I spoke at: "I've tested hundreds of moving averages and I found an 18-day moving average is as good as any of them in tracking the futures markets." Intrigued, I called him later on and he confirmed that it didn't matter too much whether you used a weighted, exponential, or simple moving average or whether you used four days, five days, or any specific number of days for the crossover average.

(Eighteen days is midway between the 16 days of trading that is necessary to create 21 days between trading events—remember the 3/21-Day Memory Law?—and the 20 trading days that constitute a lunar cycle of 28 days. I will discuss these two powerful external factors on trading later, but for the moment I just want to note that LeBeau's 18-day figure also lines up perfectly with what we might predict theoretically.)

In stocks, the total return (capital appreciation and dividends) of the S&P 500 is the benchmark for advisers and any stock system. Anyone or anything that can't outperform the total return of the S&P 500 isn't worth following. I propose an 18-day moving average standard for the futures industry.

Add up the last 18 days of trading in a specific future. Divide by 18. When that specific future closes above the 18-day moving average, buy the next opening. When it closes below the 18-day moving average, sell the next opening. Thirty days before first delivery date, start collecting closes of the next viable futures contract. When you've collected 18 days of data, switch over to the new month.

This system is simplicity itself. If you track all the major futures with it, you will find it produces many small losses that are made up by one or two huge moves (like what took place this year in coffee). In good years (like 1974 and 1980), it makes over 100 percent. In bad years (like dull 1976), it barely breaks even. But over time (I'll let you on to a dirty secret in our business), it's *net* performance is better than the vast majority of brokers, trading advisers, funds, and systems that are touted in the media.

Your only expense is a subscription to *The Wall Street Journal* (or your local paper if they have complete futures coverage). It takes only a few minutes a day to update and calculate on any computer. It's entirely unemotional and while you will take many frustrating little losses, you won't miss the big ones (like the charting expert who was urging his subscribers to go short coffee the day before the big freeze).

Because moving averages force you to stay with the trend, you rarely lose more than 1 percent of your equity even on bad trades. Finally, a moving average system limits your trading so you hardly ever violate Dull-but-Successful Futures Trading Rule #1.

Believe me, these three simple rules are worth the price of this book. The vast majority of investors would be far better off avoiding all the expensive seminars and computerized trading systems that fill up the ads. They should stick to a simple moving average system and use whatever profits and spare time they have to read everything they can get their hands on concerning the futures market.

I especially recommend the Chicago Mercantile's *Bibliography and Information Source List* as a starting point. One $5,000 loss or one $10,000 seminar can buy you a great many books. You'll find that most of "secrets of trading" are already in print at a much cheaper price than big losses or expensive seminars.

If you want to be slightly different, use openings instead of closing prices (later on I will discuss how I use opening prices). If you understand option strategy, you can use futures options instead. And, if you must, you can experiment with different types of moving averages. But until you are sure—quite sure—that you have a system that can beat this dull but profitable one I've proposed, don't bother to trade any other way.

There are some of you who have read the last few pages and are inwardly screaming, "I couldn't take this. I need to be creative, I need to be involved everyday. I want to trade full time." Okay, here's my advice to you. There is a futures exchange in Chicago called the MidAmerica Exchange. It trades smaller-sized contracts than what are traded on such exchanges as the Chicago Board of Trade, the Chicago Mercantile Exchange, the Comex, etc.

Presently the asking price for a seat on this exchange is around $6,300 (There are also a few thousand a year in fees, which are mostly waived if you do enough volume). As an exchange member, you no longer have to worry about the bid/ask slippage because you are making the market. Your commission cost is around $.50 a trade (many MidAm Clearing firms rebate part or all of your commission if you trade enough volume).

As a member of a recognized exchange, if you must trade in a contract outside the MidAm, your commissions will be around $3 at the Board of Trade and $10 at the other exchanges, not the $20–$30 of discount futures commissions. One trading technique to cover all markets would be to use a simple moving average for contracts traded outside the MidAm while you floor trade MidAm contracts.

For further information, you can call the MidAmerica Exchange in Chicago or you can call my friend Neal Weintraub at 1-800-753-7085. Neal is a member of the MidAm and for a small fee can walk you through all the steps in becoming a member, including finding you a sponsor from the exchange. Many great traders (like Richard Dennis) got their start in the mini-contracts of the MidAmerica Exchange.

Maybe you can't move to Chicago. But then you can't avoid that $45 entrance fee every time you trade a futures contract (or just about any other investment, for that matter). You are going to have to get together enough money in your account so that if you do trade every day, your trading equity isn't headed to oblivion in a very short time.

You say, "But so-and-so is trading using (software name) and making a mint." Maybe he's a terrific trader, but more likely he's just fortunate like I was during the Crash of 1987. The "Mathematics of Investing" will catch up with everyone over time. If you continue to violate them, eventually you are going to end up with the 80–90 percent who lose. At the very least you'll be like Trader Tom. You won't be able to justify all the time and energy you spend trading futures.

Follow the Winners

Before I go on to individual techniques in the futures market, I'd like to talk about the competition. There are many "How to Make a Million" in the (pick the investment)" books. Most of them are cookbooks about methods an alleged master used, or how a surefire system worked in the past.

I prefer to investigate what winning traders use now. As I see it, only 1 percent of those who trade futures make a living at it. Virtually all of them fall into three groups: floor traders (or exchange specialists), who are the masters of money management; commercials, who are the experts of the fundamentals; and those I call the insiders, the lords of high finance and the exchanges.

I don't claim this book contains every method of these successful traders or even most of them. But I tried to put down as many of their most easily applied methods as I could. I'm sure you will find something that will fit your personality and help your present trading system if you remember the first rule of investing is humility—the humility not to blame others for your trading failures, the humility to not think you are above the mathematical and psychological laws of trading, and most of all, the humility to constantly learn from others.

Chapter Three

What the
Floor Trader Knows

A client of mine was trying to sell 100,000 shares of a well-known utility stock. He had an order in to sell it, but decided he wanted to get out now. The specialist's order book showed a 100,000 buy order slightly below the price of the last trade in that stock. But when my client went to meet the bid by selling his stock to that order on the specialist's book, it suddenly disappeared. It was a phantom order never meant to be filled.

Here's the same scenario in futures. A local floor trader **A** is crying out in the bond pit "100 to buy at 104." **A** uses the hand signals that indicate that he wants to buy 100 bond contracts. Pit trader **B** turns to him and says "sold 100 at 104." Suddenly trader **A** turns to trader **B** and says, "I don't want to buy. It was a mistake."

Trader **A** won't get away with it like the phantom order-giver in the utility stock. If he doesn't relent right then, he would be hauled before a pit committee who would undoubtedly rule against him if there were any other witnesses to that transaction.

Even if no one supported Trader **B**'s complaint, the committee might still force Trader **A** to honor the trade. If he had any previous history of "chicken bids," he might be suspended or even expelled from the exchange. At the very least, he could be shunned by other pit traders who would ignore his dishonest bids and offers in favor of other traders.

That phantom utility order cost my client about $50,000. But it raised no comment in the stock market amidst the sacred specialist system. However, the financial establishment looks askance at the activities of futures floor traders.

At this point, I ought to admit my prejudices. I started in this business back in the old days when commissions were fixed by the exchanges, 24-hour trading was unheard of, and most futures pits were gentlemen's clubs that started around nine o'clock and ended just after lunch. In those days it was possible to spend hours talking to floor traders before and after trading. Virtually all of the concepts in this book had their origin in those talks. Even in these hectic times, it is still far easier to approach and have an honest discussion with a floor trader than any other consistent winner (commercial, financial insider, etc.) that trades the futures market. So I guess what I have to say is colored by hundreds of contacts with futures floor traders and my friendships with many of them. But here are the incontrovertible facts about futures floor traders:

1. *They have a level of integrity that is way above average.*

   Each day they trade billions based on fleeting, verbal contracts in the pit. Yes, many megamillion financial deals in stocks, bonds, and other financial instruments are conducted verbally strictly over the phone. Isolated cases involving stock or bond fraud don't lead the media to condemn the entire stock and bond industry. But if the occasional floor trader runs into an FBI sting, it starts another round of futures bashing.

   Many businesses in the country are heavily dependent on government subsidies. Many professions, such as doctors and lawyers, have legal monopolies that restrict entry and thereby boost costs to the consumer. The floor trader is one of the last pure entrepreneurs who asks the government for nothing but the right to stay in business without overwhelming regulation.

2. *They are absolutely essential to the economy of America.*

   The futures market, just like the stock market, can be treated like one big casino. But, like stocks, futures perform an essential economic task. They facilitate the need of producers and consumers, who don't want price fluctuations to ruin their business, to transfer the risk to someone else.

   Floor traders are responsible for over 50 percent of the trading in futures. Without them, the futures market would be illiquid and spasmodic in price movement. Futures markets would begin to dry up and fail to serve their essential economic function in our society.

   Some have called for the abolition of the open outcry system of futures, to be replaced by computerized trading where every order is matched electronically. In my opinion, this is very dangerous. There have been enough cases of computer fraud to show how easy it is to manipulate computer programs. The computerized system of NASDAQ has also been plagued with problems and a series of scandals.

   That's not to say that increased computerization can't help. I think futures trading should adopt the system already in place with the OEX option contract, where orders under 10 contracts are matched electronically and avoid the overcrowded pit. If the technology can ever be debugged, it makes sense to replace the paper cards, which floor traders use to record pit trades, with a handheld electronic device.

   But I don't want electronic trading to replace the open outcry system any more than I want Perot's Electronic Town Hall to replace the U.S. Congress. Any time you concentrate market power in the hands of the few (in this case, those who control the computer program), you are in danger. Why should futures lose one of its biggest advantages over the stock market—a truly competitive marketplace—and give a handful of people an enormous advantage, like the specialist system?

3. *Becoming a floor trader isn't a license to steal. The only ones who survive are those who truly love to trade.*

    According to exchange statistics, about half the people who trade on the floor quit after two years of trading. Not all of them go broke—many retire to trade upstairs away from the frenzy of the floor; others go on to some other business. A 50 percent washout rate after two years is a lot better than the 80–85 percent loss rate after six months, which academic studies claim to be the loss rate for the average novice futures trader. But it still doesn't suggest that everyone on the floor is making a million.

    Tom Baldwin is acknowledged as one of the biggest, if not *the* biggest, floor trader in the world. He was asked (in *Futures Industry*) if he would recommend trading as a lifetime occupation. He replied:

    > "I wouldn't do it for the money. I'd do what makes me happy. You're just going to torture yourself unless you really love to trade. Making money is not what makes it fun. Being successful makes it fun, but there's so much personal, emotional involvement in it, if you don't love to work on the emotional aspect of it, you are going to hate it. I mean understanding your own emotions. Most people only deal with the emotional aspect of losing. That really is just a minor aspect to overcome. The emotional aspect of being successful is actually more difficult. Once you're successful, you have to deal with keeping your focus, and that's a full time job I think that's why the world developed systems. You try and develop a computerized system that doesn't have feelings

and then you don't have to deal with it. You can blame the system and make adjustments."

Face it, investors. A lot of successful investing is doing the same things at the same time in the same way. The bulk of the price movement of any investment occurs in a tiny fragment of time—about 1 percent of the entire year. If you don't love what you are doing, you are going to lose your focus or become bored. Boredom, the need for a new thrill, has ruined more great traders than anything else I know.

4. *Floor traders are the ultimate world capitalists.*

The Nobel Prize-winning economist Schumpeter called capitalism creative destruction. He meant the free market was always tearing down one business or industry and replacing it with another—the free flow of capital from an area of inefficiency to an area of efficiency.

All successful investing is is learning to go with this flow of funds. Predicting the future is a nice hobby and I do try to do that as much as any analyst. But nobody really knows for sure what the next Microsoft is going to be or whether it will rain in the Midwest next May. We can guess, and they may be educated guesses, but they are still only guesses.

Standing in the pit, the floor trader is at the center of a world system of allocating money among competing investments. The flow of funds of the multitrillion-dollar world economy is taking place right before him. Millions of minds with billions of data inputs in their brains are putting their two cents' worth into the market. If the floor trader doesn't constantly keep abreast of this flow of funds, he will soon find himself as obsolete as the buggy whip manufacturer.

Futures trading 25 years ago was 95 percent agricultural. Today only around 5 percent of its volume is in agricultural markets. Ten years ago, most futures trading took place in the United States. Very soon, the over-

whelming majority of futures trading will occur overseas.

Tom Baldwin, in that same *Futures Industry* interview,
went on to remark, "We found that the markets in
Europe tend to trend very well whereas the markets
here, especially the bond market, is a difficult market to
trade long term." In other words, the same big trending
markets that built many a fortune and the reputation of
many a trading system in the United States futures market of the 1970s are now occurring overseas. But how
many "I Made a Million in Futures" books are telling
you how to place an order in London?

The only investors that are going to survive the rol-
lercoaster nineties are those who imitate the floor trader
by being prepared to go wherever the international flow
of funds is taking the world economy.

5. *Most floor traders understand that the greatest secret to investment success, outside of emotional control, is consistency.*

Remember Humble Harry? He put $1,000 a month into
a system that was making 40 percent. Let's assume he
started with $50,000 and a system that returned "only"
35 percent a year. If he continued to put in $1,000 a
month, at the end of 10 years his account would be
$1,775,049.

Compound interest is the "eighth wonder of the
world," as Baron Rothschild called it. That's why most
floor traders are delighted to earn 50 percent a year on
their capital. If they can do that consistently year after
year, in no time they will get rich. To that end they
engage in all those boring investment activities like
scalping hundreds of trades for one-tick profits or waiting for that lock trade, the sure winner that comes along
every few months.

I once heard a floor trader describe what his biggest
profit was on one trade. "It was in the early days of bond
trading. Somebody put in a massive market order to buy

a thinly traded back-month bond contact. I watched in amazement as the price was quickly bid up a whole basis point ($1,000 a contract) in a matter of seconds. I quickly ran over to where this back-month option was trading and sold a thousand contracts and than ran back to the month where I was trading and bought a thousand contracts. When market conditions returned to normal, I liquidated my spread and made almost a million dollars."

It's these types of stories that give the floor trader his "vulture" reputation. But I don't see how this is much different than meeting a sudden demand by emotional consumers for Cabbage Patch dolls. If people have to have something right now and can't wait, they are going to have to pay a premium. The only other alternative is to have the government watch every economic trade to determine, like some national nanny, whether it is fair. If it doesn't involve fraud or coercion, it's fair.

It's so much sexier to talk about a system that generates a 9.56-to-1 profit-to-loss ratio than making 35 percent a year on your money, year after year. But unless you are willing to accept this reality—like most floor traders—you are almost guaranteed to fail in investing.

6. *The floor trader understands it's not all in the numbers.*

One of the most successful floor traders, Mark Ritchie, was quoted in *Futures* magazine: "Everybody is on the hunt for a mechanical system that will make money—there's no such thing. The computer is nothing more than a very good slide rule, but all of the decisions made are human decisions. All the computer does is crunch the numbers we ask it to crunch."

Do you know that computers are banned in the pits of most exchanges? Have you ever thought how those poor slobs, the floor traders, make it without that comforting computer screen in front of them? "How come they are making more money than me I am when they don't even know what the 14-period stochastic is saying now?"

According to one estimate I read, 93 percent of traders are using price data as the basis of their trading. That's about the same percent as academic studies say lose money trading futures. Isn't about time you consider getting away from the bondage of the umpteenth computer manipulation of the Sacred Six (high, low, open, close, volume, and open interest)?

There is a service in Chicago called *Listen Only Systems*. Through a telephone or satellite link, a running commentary of what is happening in the S&P 500 pit is piped to an individual trader. This running commentary is constantly describing who is bidding or offering, the size of those bids or offers, what outside factors the pit is looking at (bond prices as they are printed on the exchange price boards, etc.). Not the least of their service is the ability to listen to the noise of the pit, which is a good barometer of the emotion and size of trading.

Why would some of the most sophisticated traders in the world pay for such a service if everything you needed to know was in that price you see on your computer screen?

Again and again floor traders have told me how much "being there" helps their trading: seeing the traders that (almost) always win and the ones that normally lose (and won't be around much longer), seeing the fear or the confidence reflected in the eyes of individual traders.

One ex-floor trader put it this way: "Guys will be yelling and carrying on, but the good floor traders will be quiet for a long time. Then the market breaks through a key point. They see opportunity *and* low risk and they pounce."

Of all the winners that truly have the trader's edge, the techniques of the floor trader are the ones the average trader can imitate the best. Of course, there are many things public speculators can't do because they are not trading at $1.00 commission rates (elaborate spread and option strategies, etc.).

But over the next few chapters I will discuss floor trading techniques that don't depend on a computer or ultra-low commissions. They may not be discussed in the media by the experts, but they are the lifeblood of people who do every day what these experts can only dream about—capture millions of dollars in trading profits.

Chapter Four

Sayings from the Floor

Up to now, I haven't discussed any of those "hot" techniques most of you bought this book for. I'm sure some have already skipped the first few chapters and are busy reading The Theory of the Opening, Fib Time Trading, etc.

I understand how the things I've written in the last chapters are like castor oil to many. They are so contrary to what you commonly hear about futures trading that I'm sure many of you are wondering, "Just who is this guy? Is this really right?"

The ancient book of wisdom says that out of two or three witnesses shall every fact be established. So I am going to give you that second witness (and a few more besides that). Read the words admired by some of the best traders that ever existed, words I call "Sayings from the Floor."

Over the years I've heard many traders discuss the markets. I've read many interviews by the big names in futures trading. Over and over again, you hear the same secrets of success, the same books mentioned, etc. So I've compiled what I call the "Big Three" of successful futures trading:

Most successful traders had someone special who helped them when they started out and showed them what to do.

If you want to be a winner, pattern yourself after somebody you know who is actually winning in the same circumstances you find yourself. What's possible for a floor trader may not be possible for a public trader who is paying that $45 initiation fee every time he or she trades. If you can't watch the market eight hours a day, you shouldn't assume the methods of your local "Joe the Daytrader" are going to be of any use to you, despite his glittering track record.

The greatest enemy of successful futures trading is trading on emotion rather than on a rational, well-executed plan.

I've never heard of or read about any big-time futures trader that didn't have at least one (usually it was more than one) horrible trading experience that made them painfully aware of this fact.

There is no bible for futures trading, but there are least three books that are cited again and again.

If you cornered a big name and asked him, "What should I read to become a successful futures trader," he would probably mumble something about reading a basic manual about futures trading (like the one the Board of Trade puts out).

That's a good answer since a great deal of mastering any profession is just knowing what people are talking about. It's amazing how people will spend years of study and thousands of dollars to become a lawyer or a doctor, but somehow they think they can enter the high-income profession of futures trader without doing a bit of preparation. Finishing school won't make you a successful lawyer or doctor, but unless you acquire a base of market knowledge, you can't possibly hope to succeed.

Again and again I've seen public traders lose tens of thousands of dollars and be none the wiser after all their time and money. They should have put that lost $10,000 into buying every futures book they could find. All that time watching prices could have been poured into a self-directed "college course" learning about the market. This wouldn't have given them the self-discipline they also need to succeed, but it would have given them knowledge, which is one side of the two-sided coin known as successful futures trading.

A basic training manual is not the simple secret of the universe that guarantees you will become a millionaire overnight. Neither is reading everything you can get your hands on, although that is a far cheaper and less painful substitute for the normally dreadful trading results of novice traders.

But for those who must have a "secret-of-success" book, when pressed, those big names do mention three books again and again. These books are no substitute for truly studying the market and learning how to control your emotions by actually trading. But they must have something special to be mentioned over and over again by successful futures traders.

The first is *Reminiscences of a Stock Operator* by Edwin Lefevre.[1] First published in 1923, it was brought back into print because it was publicly mentioned by several prominent futures traders. In my observation (probably because it has been around longer than the other two books), this is the book most often mentioned by big-name traders as influential to their careers.

The next is *Viewpoints of a Commodity Trader* by Roy Longstreet.[2] Roy was actually trading when I first started in the futures business as a broker. But he was only a name, a wispy legend, until I read an interview of him in the now defunct *Intermarket* magazine. After reading Longstreet's interview, I was inspired to read his book. I don't know if it is still in print. If you can't find it, next time you are in Chicago, stop off and read the copy housed in the Board of Trade Library.

The last book is *Market Wizards* by Jack Schwager,[3] which is a collection of interviews with well-known Chicago traders. This book deserves all the praise that's been heaped on it, although I think at least some of its success is due to what I call the "Reggie Jackson factor." Reggie was a great ballplayer when

---

1   Edwin Lefevre, *Reminiscences of a Stock Operator*, reprint of 1923 ed. (Chicago: Traders Press, 1985)
2   Roy Longstreet, *Viewpoints of a Commodity Trader* (New York: Fraser Publishing Co. 1947)
3   Jack Schwager, *Market Wizards* (New York: Simon & Schuster, 1989)

he played in Oakland, but he didn't become "Mr. October" until he played for the Yankees.

I suspect Roy Longstreet's track record was comparable to most of the *Market Wizards* interviewed by Schwager. One of Jack's wizards, Michael Steinhardt, had an awful track record in 1994. But as the denizens of the Big Apple are fond of saying, "If doesn't happen in New York, it doesn't happen."

The following are selected quotes from these books plus quotes from floor traders I have known. I call them "Sayings from the Floor" since you hear the same things again and again, repeated in different ways, from floor traders and other successful futures traders.

> "It takes a man a long time to learn all the lessons of his mistakes. They say there are two sides to everything. But there is only one side to the stock market; and it is not the bull side or bear side but the right side. It took me longer to get that principle fixed firmly in my mind than it did most of the more technical phases of the game of stock speculation."
>
> —Edwin Lefevre, *Reminiscences of a Stock Operator*

My friend Neal Weintraub heard this once from a trader: "The way to make money in this business is not to be smart, just avoid being stupid (by betting everything you have on a few trades)."

> "It never was my thinking that made the big money for me. It was always my sitting... It's no trick to be right on the market. You always find a lot of early bulls in bull markets and early bears in bear markets.... Men who can both be right and sit tight are uncommon."
>
> —Edwin Lefevre, *Reminiscences of a Stock Operator*

"When I am long with a large profit, I get into my car and leave town. At each town I come to, I call the office and reduce my position & I always took my profits too soon."

—Roy Longstreet, *Viewpoints of a Commodity Trader*

At this point, I'd like to stop and say that the last two quotes are not necessarily contradictory. Futures trading, because of the lower margin and commission rates, has a different pulse than stocks. The usual rule of thumb (as told to me by one floor trader) is: "Double your money, take your profits. If you still like the market, start a new position as if you had never made a dime."

With 5 percent down, a 5 percent move in futures doubles your money. Commissions are a tiny fraction of the underlying contract. With stocks, you must put up 50 percent margin, so you need a 50 percent move to double your money (which, due to inflation and growth, is generally easier to do in bull markets. Unfortunately, markets move down faster than they move up, even if, in percentage terms, stocks tend to go up farther than they move down).

In stocks, it doesn't make sense to take 2 percent profits when your commissions (in and out) are 2 percent. You must have the patience to wait for those 50 percent (usually) up moves. In futures, you need the discipline to get out when you've doubled your initial stake and not yield to greed. You can't pyramid a winning position by violating the Psychological Law of 10/20 Percent—which is very easy to do when the market moves in your direction. Or, as Longstreet put it:

"A good general never risks all of his troops in the front line at one time."

—Roy Longstreet, *Viewpoints of a Commodity Trader*

"The average man doesn't wish to be told that this is a bull or bear market. What he desires is to be told specifically which particular stock to buy or sell. He wants to get something for nothing. He doesn't want to work. He doesn't even wish to have to think. It is too much bother to count the money that he picks up from the ground."

—Edwin Lefevre, *Reminiscences of a Stock Operator*

"People don't want to learn how to trade. They want to be told what to do."

—Common floor saying

"A loss never bothered me after I take it. I forget it overnight. But being wrong—and not taking the loss— that is what does the damage to the pocketbook and to the soul."

—Edwin Lefevre, *Reminiscences of a Stock Operator*

"The greatest loss is self-confidence."

—Roy Longstreet, *Viewpoints of a Commodity Trader*

"The speculator's chief enemies are always boring from within. It is inseparable from human nature to hope and to fear. In speculation when the market goes against you, you hope that every day will be the last day—and you lose more than you should had you not listened to hope—to the same ally that is a potent success-bringer to empire builders and pioneers, big and little. And when the market goes your way you become fearful that the next day will take away your profit, and you get out—too soon. Fear keeps you from making as much money as you ought to. The success-ful trader has to fight these two deep-seated instincts.

He has to reverse what you might call his natural impulses.... He must fear that his loss may develop into a much bigger loss and hope that his profit may become a big profit."

—Edwin Lefevre, *Reminiscences of a Stock Operator*

Another old floor trader saying, as quoted in *Market Wizards*, reads, "Put stops where they can't be reached (easily)." The idea is to make sure your analysis (at least temporarily) was bad if you are stopped out. That way you won't pull your stops or immediately reenter the market on the same side without stepping back and analyzing the situation afresh.

Market Wizards also contains another common saying: "We don't trade markets, we trade money."

"That is one trouble about trading on a large scale. You cannot sneak out as you can when you pike along. You cannot always sell out when you wish or when you think it wise. You have to get out when you can, when you have a market that will absorb your entire line. Failure to grasp the opportunity to get out may cost you millions. You cannot hesitate. If you do you are lost."

—Edwin Lefevre, *Reminiscences of a Stock Operator*

"The big players always tip their hand."

—Michael Marcus, as quoted in *Market Wizards*

"A market can and often does cease to be a bull market long before prices generally are ready to break. My long expected warning came to me when I noticed that, one after another, those stocks which had been the leaders of the market...did not come back."

—Edwin Lefevre, *Reminiscences of a Stock Operator*

"Three drives to a top" is another common floor saying I heard long before R.N. Elliott. By the way, the three drives to a top of a commodity bull are quite different than those of a stock bull (more on this later).

"I like the short side of the market because there is less company."

—Roy Longstreet, *Viewpoints of a Commodity Trader*

Consider this facetious floor trader saying: "When you're long, you're wrong." This saying contains these kernels of truth: bear markets go down faster than bull markets, and during the start and middle of bull markets, selling points are usually easier to identify than buying spots.

"Observation, experience, memory, and mathematicsthese are what the successful trader must depend on. He must not only observe accurately but remember at all times what he has observed.... He must always rely on probabilities—that is, try to anticipate them. Years of practice at the game, of constant study, of always remembering, enable the trader to act on the instant when the unexpected happens as well as when the expected comes to pass."

—Edwin Lefevre, *Reminiscences of a Stock Operator*

The worse the fills are, the better the trade.

—Bruce Kovner as quoted in *Market Wizards*

"Now, ordinarily a man ought to be able to buy and sell a million bushels of wheat within a range of 1/4 cent. On this day when I sold 250,000 bushels to test the market for timeliness, the price went down 1/4 cent. Then, since the reaction did not definitely tell me all I wished to know, I sold another quarter of a million bushels...the price went down 1-1/2 cents on my selling.... Such being the case, what was the only thing to do? Of course, to sell a lot more. Following the dictates of experience may fool you, now and then. But not following them invariably makes an ass of you. So I sold 2 million bushels and the price went down more. A few days later the market's behavior practically compelled me to sell an additional 2 million bushels and the price declined further still; a few days later wheat started to break badly and slumped off six cents...."

—Edwin Lefevre, *Reminiscences of a Stock Operator*

Two more common sayings are: "The best charts are the ones you never see," and "You're never far from (take your pick): a Gann Line, an Elliott Wave Extension, a tech point, etc."

Ninety percent of traders are taught to look at two basic indicators: momentum measures (like stochastics, RSI, percent R, etc.) and chart formations. Since 90 percent are losing, maybe it's time for you to find the charts you never see running in *Investor's Business Daily* and stop looking for some esoteric reason why you lost ("I missed this Gann line," ad nauseum) in the charts you do see.

"Every time you tell somebody what you know, you sell yourself on its importance."

—Roy Longstreet, *Viewpoints of a Commodity Trader*

"Trading is like baseball. Winning is 90 percent defense and knowing when to swing for a three-run homer. If you strike out, remember Ruth struck out more than he homered."

—Floor trader speaking to me years ago

"Traders often enter the 'Hall of Mirrors'... They see only success (wherever they look)."

—Roy Longstreet, *Viewpoints of a Commodity Trader*

"Yesterday's hero, today's goat" is an old floor trader adage repeated to me in many forms (a good thing to remember when you see the next George Soros touted to the skies by the media).

On that note, I better stop. I could go on and on. Get those three books, read them yourself, and take a small step on the long road that leads to successful futures investing.

Chapter Five

The Theory of the Opening

For years I've been speaking at Neal Weintraub's seminars here in Chicago. Neal founded *Commodity Boot Camp*, sold it, and now runs the "Tricks of the Trader" seminars. There is one thing Neal does at every seminar I've seen: After a weekend of teaching sessions, Neal takes his attendees to watch Monday's opening in the grain pits at the Board of Trade. After the frenzy of the opening, Neal points out that about half the traders get off the floor and take a break. You can actually hear the decrease in the noise from the pit. By 10:00 A.M., half an hour after the opening, some days it seems you could shoot off a gun in the middle of these grain pits and not hit anyone.

This phenomenon is most visible in the grain pits, but it also occurs in varying degrees in every other trading pit I have ever seen. Virtually every floor trader that is not on vacation seems to be there on the opening. That's not the case during other trading hours. Even the close often finds many floor traders on the sideline or already home.

Back in the days when futures trading was basically a 9:00 A.M.-to-1:00 P.M. gentlemen's club, a lot of us brokers would stumble in around 8:00 A.M. and complain bitterly about how lucky stockbrokers were. Their market opened at 10:00 A.M. instead of the ungodly 8:30 A.M. of silver. For a long time, it never ceased to amaze me that many floor traders who cleared through our firm had come in hours earlier; some as early as 4:00 A.M.!

After calling half the country to find out market conditions and thinking about the markets for hours, many of the same floor traders would still get to the pit early, sometimes hours before the opening bell, just so they could get a good position to execute orders on the opening. Then we would often see these same early risers, a half hour after the opening, back up in their offices, often joking, and quite willing to talk to us peon brokers.

I learned many a good trading technique during these mid-session breaks as floor traders would talk with one eye on the screen and one eye on me. Occasionally, they would see some price movement and say, "That looks interesting," and go back on the floor. But most of the time they would do one of two things: Go home, or come back to the market at a regular time, notably at 11:00 A.M., the start of the New York lunch hour. (Break times vary with markets. Bond traders usually want to be around during Fed intervention time from 10:20 to 10:50 A.M. CST.)

Why would these men, who paid big bucks for a seat and spent enormous time preparing for the market opening, be so willing to leave their livelihood early, sometimes after only a few minutes of trading? Why were they so often cavalier about the close, which everyone "knows" is the most important event of the trading day?

One explanation could be the Psychological Law of 10/20 Percent. We have 168 hours in a week. Ten percent of 168 hours is 16.8 hours; 20 percent is 33.6 hours. The average worker officially puts in about 33.6 hours per week after break time, vacations, and sick leave are taken out.

But actually, much of our society's work (especially in government institutions) is "F&S"—faking and stretching work to fill out the time before 5:00 P.M. Some 16.8 hours a week of real work may be a generous estimate of what workers actually do. They so resent the time they are forced to work, an agent's 10 percent is all the effort they can muster up.

Even people who love their work will find it hard to sustain all-out hours of work much beyond 20 percent of the week. They might begin to suffer serious fatigue and burn out. In short, after hours preparing for the strain of a market opening, even the most committed floor traders might need a break shortly after the opening.

But this still doesn't explain all this emphasis on the opening. Why don't floor traders come into the pit during the middle of the day (when the other floor traders are off the floor resting), claim a good position in the pit to execute trades, and stay for the rest of the trading day? If six hours a day, 30 hours a week is about all the quality hours anyone can put into his or her job, why don't S&P 500 floor traders, to give an example, waltz in about an hour after the opening at 9:30 A.M., put in their six hours, and quit after the "all-important" closing bell at 3:15 P.M.?

Then it dawned on me. How many hours do the markets trade? How many hours do they not trade? Don't events that move markets occur all the time, seven days a week?

What does the close reflect? A few hours of price exploration, which might not reflect any major external or internal event that would influence the long-term trend of the market. What does the opening reflect? Doesn't it reflect the accumulated wisdom, the market events of many more hours of human existence? Which is more important in terms of potential market movement? The trading decisions made and events that occur during the up to 68 hours (on a weekend) when a future is closed, or the few hours the future is trading?

Even 24-hour trading in currencies has gaps in trading hours. There is an hour or two between the close of the New York markets and the start of Asian trading in Sydney. And then there is the long hiatus between the end of New York trading on Friday and the start of Asian trading on Sunday night U.S. time. Which is a more important price? The close of New York trading, with only 22 hours of continuous trading behind it, or the opening of Asia Sunday night, the first time the currency market can speak after a rest of about 50 hours?

Think of it this way. Measure the size of the closing range (the price movement of the last 30 seconds in trading). Measure the price movement of the opening range (the first 30 seconds in trading). You will probably find on average they are similar, with a slight edge in volatility usually going to the opening range. But if you measure price movement between the close and the extreme quote (up or down versus the close) in the opening range, you will suddenly find the opening range winning hands down in the volatility race with the closing range.

Even the most novice trader is warned about those instruments of devastation, the dreaded commodity reports, the USDA Pig-Crop Report that will trap you for days in limit moves, or the unemployment report that causes half your bond equity to disappear in a single minute.

But what is an opening but a report? Every trading day, at the opening, the market makes its report on what happened overnight. Every opening (except the relatively rare "split opening" where there is no price movement from yesterday's close) is a time of rejoicing for some and weeping for others. It's the moment of truth when cheap talk is finished and every participant has to put up or shut up and make his bids and offers.

What is the usual worst case scenario after a Pig Crop Report? A $1,000 limit move against you in hogs? $1,500? Yet investors think nothing of losing $100 or $200 on the hog opening, day after day, week after week, month after month. Every morning they say to themselves, "I don't need to worry. The market will go back my way again." Panicked in front of the big reports, they are suffering the death of a thousand cuts from the little "reports" of each day's opening.

It's the fear of what the opening will bring that causes many to daytrade and never hold a futures position overnight. But there's two big problems for the public with this approach . One is that average $45 initiation fee for every contract you trade. The other is the loss of volatility so necessary for public speculators to even up the odds with their professional rivals.

A floor trader can make money with one-tick trading. If he buys the bid and sells the offer and pockets a one-tick profit in cattle of $10.00, his only expenses are about $1.00 in clearing fees and whatever the interest cost of his seat (in loans or opportunity costs) turns out to be on a single trade (the year-to-year percentage increase in the price of exchange seats has been greater than the cost of borrowing over the last 25 years, basically making this expense practically nothing).

Of course, even a floor trader doesn't always buy the bid or sell the offer. If he is wrong about the direction of the market, he might be forced to (just like the public trader) get in and out at any price he can get. But let's say he is buying the bid and selling the offer half the time he trades. The other half of the time he has to pay that same one-tick price to enter and exit that the public pays. That averages out to a $6.00 cost every time he trades.

Let's say cattle's daily range averages 50 cents a day, or $200. The floor trader's average cost per trade versus the daily range is 6-to-200, or a 3 percent daily ratio of costs to potential profits per contract. The public speculator's cost per trade is $35 (one tick of $10.00 plus $25.00 in commissions and exchange fees). His fixed cost to potential profit ratio is 35-to-200, or 17.5 percent.

Now let us assume that cattle's price range from the previous close to the extreme of today's high or low (depending on which is greater) averages out to be 75 points, or $300. If the public speculator buys or sells on yesterday's close and offsets it some time during today's trading, that decreases the cost to potential profit ratio to 35-to-300, or 11.66 percent, a 50 percent decrease over daytrading alone.

In order for the public trader to get down to the 3 percent ratio of the floor trader, he must look for potential swings in price action totaling $1,167 from top to bottom. A $1,167 swing in cattle trading happens, on average, every few weeks. (This is exactly what following a standard moving average like our 18-day example does. A public trader is forced to take only trades that fit the 3 percent ratio of potential profit to fixed costs of daytrading floor traders).

Still not convinced the opening is a more important price than the close? According to a book by R. Earl Hadady (the father of contrary opinion futures trading), the opening is more likely to be near the low or high of the day than the close. (Opening Price Statistical Data, 1984.)

Listen up, daytraders. If you are not prepared for the opening, if you don't make that the focus of your trading instead of the close, you are going to lose a great deal of the potential profit that there is in each day's trading.

You see, the close is just a bookkeeping entry. It's just a convenient way to give the back office a chance to catch up and everyone a chance to get some rest. The strong hands of the market know that, about 60 percent of the time, if the opening is higher, the close is going to be higher. In other words, most of the time the opening has already told the professionals what they can expect at the end of the day, and they plan their trading accordingly.

It's only the weak hands, the dumb money, that hold out to the close, hoping for some miracle reversal to save them. When it doesn't, like the majority of the time, they go on margin call and are forced out. Even if there is a last-minute miracle reversal, these poor slobs might still be long gone, forced out by their broker well before the close because their intraday account balance went near zero and their credit with their broker was already used up.

I have one last appeal for all you technicians out there. Why were candlestick charts all the rage the last few years? Isn't the secret of the Orient the opening? What is the essential ingredient that makes all those hammers and clouds different from standard Western bar charts? Isn't it fact that the opening is used to draw the candle body? Aren't candlesticks just a much overdue admission that the opening is at least the equal of the close in determining market direction?

By the way, do any of those hotlines you spend good money on use open-only stops? Does your hotshot computer system weight the opening price more than the closing price in its decisions? Does it even input the opening price? Is the chart you see also missing the opening?

Ninety percent of futures traders don't give a second thought to the opening. Ninety percent of futures traders are losing. Isn't there a strong correlation between these two statistics?

Floor Trading Opening Systems

The opening is not only a report, it is usually a gap. The opening price range normally does not touch or include prices from the previous night's closing range. This may be a common gap, but it is a gap nonetheless. And just as we would expect from technical theory, usually there is an immediate attempt to close the gap on the part of the markets. Floor traders call this "fading the opening."

For the first 10 seconds or so of the opening, usually there are no trades consummated. Bids and offers are made until one bid and one offer finally meet. This feeling-out process is critical to the way the floor trader will act during the rest of the opening.

Normally, he will not bid or offer on the opening until the market uncovers a big bid or big offer. Then he will step in front of this order by bidding one tick below (if it is an offer) or one tick above (if it is a bid). If the market appears to be against the direction of his order, he can dump his order safely into the arms of that waiting bid or offer. Like every professional, and unlike the public, the floor trader is always more concerned about minimizing his losses than he is about being right.

Here's an example. The opening range in November soybeans is 6.03 to 6.04. It immediately moves up to 6.04 1/2 where a big commercial is attempting to sell a few million bushels. The previous closing range was 5.99 1/2 to 6.00 1/2, or 6.00 settlement. Our floor trader will sell his November beans at 6.04 1/4, a tick below the big order to sell at 6.04 1/2.

His expectation is that the market will fade and attempt to close the gap created by the bottom of the opening range at 6.03 and the top of the closing range at 6.00 1/2. If he sees that the market is acting too strong, he can buy in his short sale using the commercial order at 6.04 1/2. If he didn't have that big order, he might have to pay 6.04 3/4, 6.05, or even higher to get out of his position as the market surged up with little selling.

This fading action is normal because public traders, who are usually long, normally have an irresistible impulse to take profits whenever they are the tiniest bit ahead. Even when the market opens lower, there is a tendency by the public to double up and buy some more "bargains." Any public trader that is short, like his long counterparts, will tend to take profits and help force the market up.

"Public time" varies slightly with every market. In gold, it peaks during the New York lunch hour, from 11:10 to 11:50 A.M. CST. In the agricultural markets, we have the "Noon Balloon," where farmers call their broker after listening to the noon agricultural (ag) report on their radio and tell them to "Texas hedge," which means to go long in the market when they already have plenty to sell of the same thing on their farm.

Commercials and floor traders are not stupid. They know this is the normal pattern. If they are bullish, they will wait until public profit-taking has battered prices back to the closing range or some other technical or fundamental buying point. If they want to sell, they do the opposite. If they are so eager to sell or buy that they don't wait for this routine of the market, that is very significant for future price action. (I'll discuss this later.)

The gap created by the opening from the closing price is easily observed on an intraday price chart that extends over several days trading. You can use a 30-minute bar chart as you would a daily chart and do all the technical tricks chartists do with gaps. Since less people look at intraday charts than daily charts, you will have a greater chance of being right in using standard gap technical analysis.

Gap analysis is in every book on charting. Since I promised myself this book would be about techniques rarely if ever discussed, I'll confine myself to saying that most gaps created by the action of the opening are closed within a few days, since about 85 percent of the time markets are not trending strongly in one direction or another.

If you call your broker up or if you have some sort of service that pipes in news about the futures market to your place of trading, you can usually get the "opening call." This opening call can be a powerful signal, especially if you are trading a primary market.

There are many places that trade currencies, but the primary markets are the big banks in New York and London. Soybeans are traded in Osaka and Rotterdam, but the primary market is in Chicago. London trades U.S. stocks, but the bulk of the trading is in New York.

Based on the latest prices in Rotterdam, soybeans are expected to rise 10 cents immediately on the opening. If soybeans are only up five cents on the opening, that is a powerful sell signal. Either somebody wants to get out of beans so badly they are willing to forego $250 a contract in profit to get out, and/or the demand that pushed up the thin Rotterdam market is not enough to get the much bigger market in Chicago moving.

This works exactly in reverse for a lower opening. A market that was called 10 cents lower and opens five cents lower has given a strong signal to buy. (No, this doesn't always work, but hopefully if you read the first chapters in my book, you are never going to be tempted by "bet-the-ranch" trading.)

The Split Opening

Still another opening routine is the split opening. This works best in the agricultural markets, but it is worth noting wherever it happens in a primary market. A split opening is when the opening range is inside or identical to the previous closing range.

When a market opens within a tick of the close, it signifies a lack of fresh overnight fundamentals. The market then is driven purely by technical factors. It should trade below and above the opening range.

On Figure 5-1, you can see that the June 22, 1994 opening of July beans was almost identical to the June 21, 1994 July bean close (A). The July bean June 21 closing range was 6.78–6.75. The

Figure 5-1

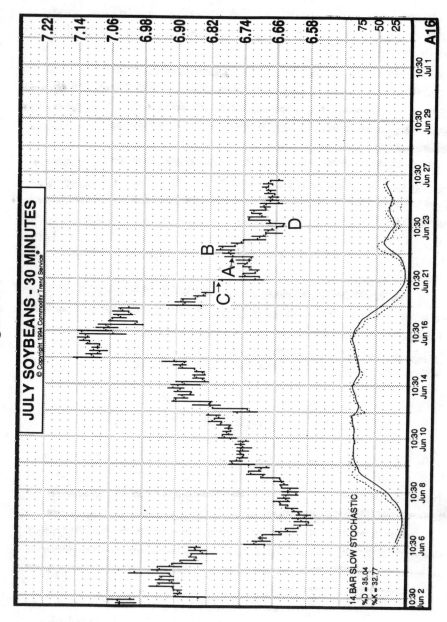

JULY SOYBEANS - 30 MINUTES
© Copyright 1994 Commodity Trend Service

14 BAR SLOW STOCHASTIC
%D = 35.04
%K = 32.77

7.22
7.14
7.06
6.98
6.90
6.82
6.74
6.66
6.58
75
50
25

A16

10:30 Jun 2 | 10:30 Jun 6 | 10:30 Jun 8 | 10:30 Jun 10 | 10:30 Jun 14 | 10:30 Jun 16 | 10:30 Jun 21 | 10:30 Jun 23 | 10:30 Jun 27 | 10:30 Jun 29 | 10:30 Jul 1

© Copyright 1994 Commodity Trend Service

next day's opening range for July beans was 6.76 1/2 and 6.78.

The opening range is "enclosed," or inside the closing range; in other words, at no point does the July bean June 22 opening range exceed the high or low of the closing range on June 21 for the July bean contract. This enclosed or identical relationship of the opening range to the previous closing range is the classic split opening.

The floor broker who first taught me about split openings told me he paid off his mortgage and his daughter's education using the split opening technique I am going to illustrate below. But he also told me you could wait quite a while before a split opening occurred.

From my experience, if the opening range extends one tick above or below the previous closing range, this may not be the classic split opening, but you can still trade it as such. The increased opportunity to trade the split opening more than makes up for the increase in risk. But I wanted you to know this opening routine exactly as it was told to me.

After the split opening (Figure 5-1, A), you wait to see which way the market breaks out of the opening range, which in the case of our example was to the upside. The market will then travel to the next zone of resistance or support and then stop and reverse.

There is no exact science on what this next zone is, but it's usually easy to see on a chart. In this case, the market rallied to just above 6.80, (Figure 5-1, B) the top of the previous day's range and right in the middle of an unfilled chart gap (Figure 5-1, C). After reversing at the zone of resistance or support, the market will go through the opening range to the next zone of resistance or support after the opening range.

If the market breaks out to the upside, as in our example, sometime during the day it will reverse at a zone (in our example of resistance) and go back under the opening range (Figure 5-1, D) to another zone (in this case of support). If there is an immediate downside breakout from the opening range, you buy the next support and wait for the market to reverse, go through the opening range on the upside, and then you take your profit at the next resistance.

In our example, the market went through the first support, under the opening range at 6.70, all the way to 6.64. This is typical for a split opening in a trending market, in this case a bear market. This extra daily action is a perfect illustration of how I think most traders should use the split opening.

The split opening was originally developed as a floor trader daytrade system. Given proper risk management, you might—I repeat *might*—be able to make money off it trading this method off the floor. But I prefer you use it as another tool in getting aboard a trend: It gave you another reason to sell at 6.80 and hop aboard a profitable trend that would eventually take July beans to 6.55 within a week.

Initial/Maintenance Opening Indicator

By far the most powerful trading signal generated on the opening is when the normal fade-the-opening action doesn't appear. If these two techniques don't break your fixation with the close, nothing will.

Remember the old floor trader saying, "We don't trade markets, we trade money?" Professional traders, unlike the losing public, rarely use all their available speculative assets in their trading account.

In the first place, it's psychologically comforting to know if you lose 10 percent of your trading account, it's really not 10 percent of your liquid assets. In addition, the interest paid on margin money held by a clearing firm is rarely more than 90 percent of the current T-bill rate, which is definitely not the highest rate you can get safely on liquid assets. It's quite simple to transfer money from a higher-yielding liquid asset account to your trading account whenever you need money.

This interest rate differential can be substantial if you are carrying a $1+ million cash balance as many floor traders do.

This creates an incentive to put as little as possible in your trading account.

When you put up margins in futures, you have a minimum initial margin you must put up as soon as you carry a trade overnight. In soybeans, that was around $1,350 a contract during the recent run-up in prices in May and June 1994. If you put up just that amount, you could hold that single contract as long as your day-ending account balance was over $1,000 (the maintenance margin). If you lost more than $350, or seven cents per contract, you would be required to bring your account back up to the initial margin of $1,350.

Let's say a floor trader was long May soybeans over the long weekend of April 1 to April 3. The previous close on March 31 was 681 3/4 (Figure 5-2, A). The opening on April 4 was 676, a $275 loss (Figure 5-2, B). Immediately, our floor trader is in danger of having to come up with more money to maintain his position.

All his monetary incentives (as well as standard risk management) say he should get out now. He also knows that a Monday opening after a three-day weekend is the "king" of prices, a powerful signal in itself. He sells his long out and goes with the flow of the market by selling.

On the other hand, Farmer John is a typical futures trader who has read the newspaper stories about the shortage of beans and "knows" his soybeans have to go up. If he doesn't buy more, he is going to try to ride out this temporary fall in his beloved bean position. When does he get out? Usually when his money runs out! That's the rationale behind the *Initial-Maintenance Opening Rule.*

The margin on beans is $1,350, or 27 cents. If Farmer John bought the March 31 close of 681 3/4 in the May beans, his money would run out at 6.44 3/4. But Farmer John probably wanted to get an early start on the weekend. The average price he paid is somewhere in the middle of the March 31 range of 6.89 1/4 to 6.80 1/2, or around 6.85.

Note that 27 cents from 6.85 is 6.48 (Figure 5-2, C), which

Figure 5-2

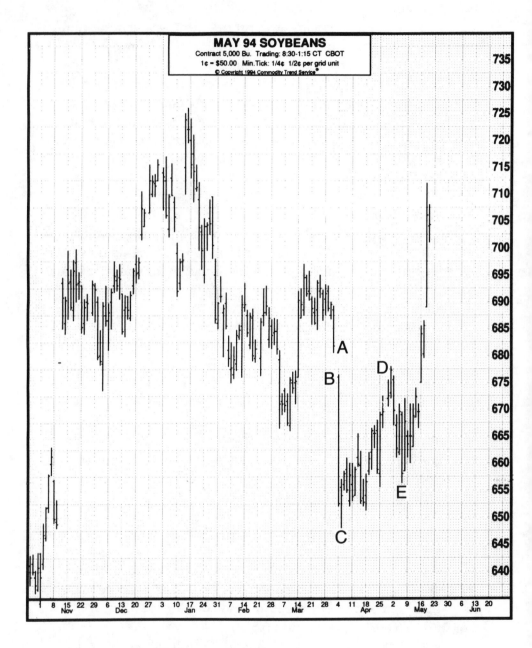

was the exact low made the next day—a low that held in the nearby bean contract for two-and-a-half months!

To sum up, the Initial-Maintenance Opening Rule states:

If in the first few minutes of trading a market moves up or down from the midpoint of the previous day's range (or the previous close if the previous day's range was huge) by a sum equal to or greater than the difference between initial and maintenance margin, it sets up a minimum objective equal to the middle of the range of the previous day's trading minus or plus the initial margin, depending on the direction of the move begun on that opening.

We see this same principle in early June in the July soybeans (Figure 5-3).

The July beans (A) closed at 700 1/2 on June 1. It opened at 6.90 (B) on June 2. The projected low would be 27 cents below the middle of the June 1 range of July beans (6.99 1/2), or 6.72 1/2. Despite the raging bull market, this objective was reached on the June 6 opening of 6.70 in July beans (C).

On June 14, July beans closed at 6.90 1/2 (D). The next day opening was at 7.10 (E). The objective would have been 27 cents higher than the midpoint of the June 12 range of July beans, or 7.14 3/4. The high of June 15 was 7.15.

On June 20, July beans closed at 6.81 and opened the next day at 6.75 (F). The middle of the June 20 range in July beans was 6.86 3/4, giving us an objective of 6.59 3/4, which was reached on June 27 (G).

When this opening technique fails, it is a powerful signal that a trend change is imminent. On June 15, July beans closed at 7.05 3/4 and opened the next day at 7.13(H). The objective predicted by this action would be 7.36. Instead of moving toward this figure, beans closed lower that day.

The next day trading day was a Friday. In a bull market, only the strongest hands can stomach going short over a weekend. There should have been a powerful up move. beans had been moving around 20–30 cents in one direction or another every two days. Yet July beans never even got close to the 7.36 objective, failing to penetrate the 7.15 high set two days before.

Figure 5-3

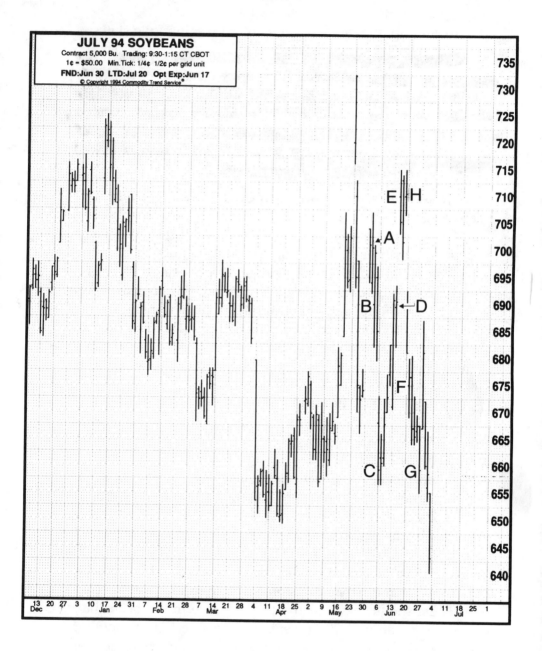

JULY 94 SOYBEANS
Contract 5,000 Bu. Trading: 9:30-1:15 CT CBOT
1¢ = $50.00   Min.Tick: 1/4¢ 1/2¢ per grid unit
FND:Jun 30 LTD:Jul 20   Opt Exp:Jun 17
© Copyright 1994 Commodity Trend Service®

Yes, this Initial-Maintenance Opening Rule is a powerful tool, especially in a primary market like the U.S. grain pits. But there is even a more powerful opening indicator, which is the topic of the next section.

Open to the Up, Open to the Down

In our first example above in May beans, if you take a look at Figure 5–2, B, you will see that the high of April 4 was made on the opening. This is not normal. The normal pattern is for the market to rally beyond the top of the opening range and test some big resting order above the market that the locals have discovered on the opening and are trying to fade. When a market makes its high on the opening, the floor trader who first described it to me called it an "open to the up."

I've tried to think of a better name. But when you think about it, this formation is an open technical formation that hasn't been closed by subsequent market action that took prices above the top of this opening range. The opposite formation, where the low is made during the opening range, is called an "open to the down."

The next step is to apply the *Rule of Three*. To put it in the words of the floor trader who told it to me: three minutes, three hours, three days, three weeks, three months, three years. If a gap stays open three minutes, the market will go in the direction of the gap what it would normally be expected to move in three hours. If this gap stays open longer than three hours, the future will travel in the direction of the gap what previous action would consider a normal three-day swing in prices. After three days, it would be three weeks, etc.

The Rule of Three is based on the same 3/21-Day Memory Law I outlined earlier. Markets are dominated by three- and 21-day pulses as they go from one fading memory (a report, a government action, a frost, etc.) to another more recent event. Only the 28-day moon cycle has the same impact on human trading emotions. (Three months is a quarter, the basic unit of the corporation. Three years is close to the 3.45-year Kitchin cycle, which seems to be the basic economic cycle in the world economy.)

Every technician understands that chart gaps are a directional signal. A market that gaps higher is headed higher, theoretically a certain distance based on the midpoint of the gap, the size of the leg in prices that proceeded it, etc. When an opening is the high or low in the day, that's also a gap, a break in the normal pattern of fade-the-opening trading.

Let's go back to our May bean chart (see Figure 5-2) and use the Rule of Three. After the few minutes of trading on April 4, it would have been obvious that the opening was going to be the high for the first part of trading (the three-hour time frame takes us through the noon balloon of small agricultural traders). Soybeans had been averaging around six cents in movement for every three hours of trading, which would give us a 6.76 price objective (the previous close of 6.81 1/2 minus six cents).

However, the opening price was 6.76 (some floor traders might have attempted to use the Rule of Three to scalp the opening and instead got caught trading against a powerful down move). When this level was immediately breached on the opening, the next increment, three days, would be brought into play. The last three days of action in soybeans had seen a total range of around 12 cents, or a price objective of around 6.70.

When this level went down decisively later in the day, the three-week objective was the next projected level of support. The range of the last three weeks was around 32 cents, setting up an objective of 6.50, which was almost reached that same day. (At this point, I should explain I am not using just the last three weeks of May beans, but the last three weeks of the closest-to-cash future. March beans were the spot bean contract during part of this time, and so I am using its highs and lows as part of my three-week range of bean prices).

Another open to the up occurred in July beans on May 25 (Figure 5–4, A). The opening was also the high at 6.98. Since this high was greater than the previous close, we will use that to measure our objective. The previous day had seen the July soy-

Figure 5-4

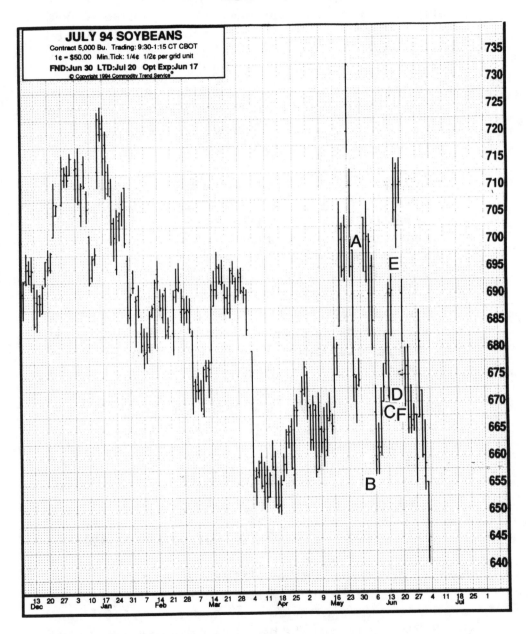

bean contract plunge 39 1/4 cents. Eighty percent of 39 1/4 (three hours is about 80 percent of the time the soybean market is open) is 31 1/4 cents, and 31 1/4 cents from the opening of 6.98 on May 25 would give us a goal of 6.66 3/4—almost identical to the 6.66 low reached the next day on May 26 (B).

An open to the down occurred on June 9 in the July beans (C). The low of the day was made on the opening at 6.70. Based on the previous close of 6.67 3 3/4 and the previous day's range of prices of 12 1/2 cents, that would give a three-hour objective of 6.77 3/4 near the high of that day.

Two days later, the market attempted to close the gap created by the open to the up at 6.70. It opened at 6.71 (D) and made a low of 6.70 1/2 and then sprang up straight. The three-day rule would give us an objective of 6.90 1/4 (22 cent range plus the previous gap close of 6.67 3/4). When this level was decisively broken on June 15 (E), the three-week objective was 7.18 1/4 (6.67 3/4 plus the 50 1/2 cent range of the last three weeks).

That's not quite the high of the move of 7.15 made that day, but it was one more piece of evidence to add to the failure of the Initial-Maintenance Opening Rule that this soybean move was almost over.

When an open to the down or an open to the up is filled (that is, the market finally goes lower than the open to the up or higher than the open to the down), there is almost always a sharp reversal right after this happens.

The 6.76 open to the down on April 4 was finally filled when the May beans went to 6.78 on April 29 (Figure 5–2, D). Immediately May beans fell, eventually reaching 6.56 1/4 on May 5 (Figure 5–2, E).

The open to the up at 6.98 of the July beans on May 25 was filled when July beans opened at 7.04 on June 1. That was the high of that day, and July beans fell to 6.92 the next day.

The open to the down of June 6 at 6.70 in the July beans was filled on June 21, when July beans made a low of 6.69 (Figure 5–4, F). Despite the powerful bear market that would carry soybeans a dollar lower a month later, the July beans never looked back and rallied straight to 6.80 1/2 the next day.

At this point, you probably think I am deliberately looking for the best examples of these previous two opening techniques. Actually, I just used the first examples I could find over the last few months.

Yes, I did look first at the most likely suspect to find examples—a bull market in grains that was full of volatility and unsophisticated traders. But all I can say is that these techniques work more often than not in any primary market. Try it yourself on many different markets. You'll wonder how you traded before you knew about these opening techniques.

The opening is the most important price of the day. That's why those floor traders could take a break after it occurred. They knew what was probably going to happen the rest of the day. They already had made their money (or at the very least had taken a minimum amount of losses).

So apply the same opening techniques the floor traders use and take a break, like they do, from the screen. In my opinion, freedom from the tyranny of always having to watch the screen is worth just as much to you as any technique I write about.

Chapter Six

The Routine
of the Market

If you went to college, perhaps you were forced like I was to sit through some required Psych 101 class. To this day, I am suspicious of what passes for psychology. But I do remember one classic experiment.

A number of people are put into a room with a psychologist. All but one are "ringers" put there by the psychologist, and the unsuspecting individual is seated last away from the psychologist. In this room is a film screen. A picture is flashed on the screen of two sticks. One is slightly, but clearly, longer than the other.

The psychologist then asks the ringers: "Are these sticks the same size?" All around the room each of the ringers say "Yes." What do you think the poor slob who wasn't in on the trick said? Most of the time he or she said, "Yes," too! Testing showed this phenomena became quite strong after eight ringers had answered and leveled out after 12 ringers had said their lying "Yesses."

I often think of the public futures trader as that poor slob. He's always being confused into thinking $2 + 2 = 5$. It's not that he is being lied to all the time. It's just that his ignorance of market realities and his constant emotions of greed and fear blind him to the profit opportunities that are all around him.

The floor trader and other professional futures traders are like that rare but brave soul who, in the psychology experiment, might say "No. I don't care what the rest are saying. One stick is longer than the other." They trust their own experience and judgment.

Ninety percent are losing because they are looking for something simple that will turn a "tiny into a trillion," as one of my friends likes to say. The pros are quite content to make a little at a time consistently or, as the old floor trader adage puts it, "Nickels turn into millions if you are picking them up all the time."

Floor traders and other professionals primarily feast on two market conditions: the opportunities and trading direction they find on the opening, and the routine of the market. By routine of the market, I mean trading conditions that repeat themselves over and over again at predictable intervals.

One routine is fairly well-known: seasonal patterns, or sure-thing trading, as it is called in some circles. Most people have seen the ads or read the books " buy February bellies at the close on X date and sell them on Y Date, because this has worked 100 percent of the time since the winter of 1966," etc.

Titles like "sure-thing trading" turn me off, but that doesn't mean seasonal trading is not a powerful tool. Nine years out of 10, corn and beans are going to fall in price during July. There is a February break that occurs in late winter among grain prices. Bonds tend to rally during the first two weeks of June, etc.

Now that daily seasonal probabilities are everywhere (see Figure 6-1), this tool may be losing its punch. By all means, you should consider seasonal tendencies when you make your trading decisions. But remember, any technique that everybody knows can be ruined by too many people trying to use it.

Floor traders and commercials are well aware of seasonal factors. When the thundering herd comes into buy that sure-thing trade, they just step aside and let the herd bid up prices to the moon. When everything comes back to earth and the

Figure 6–1

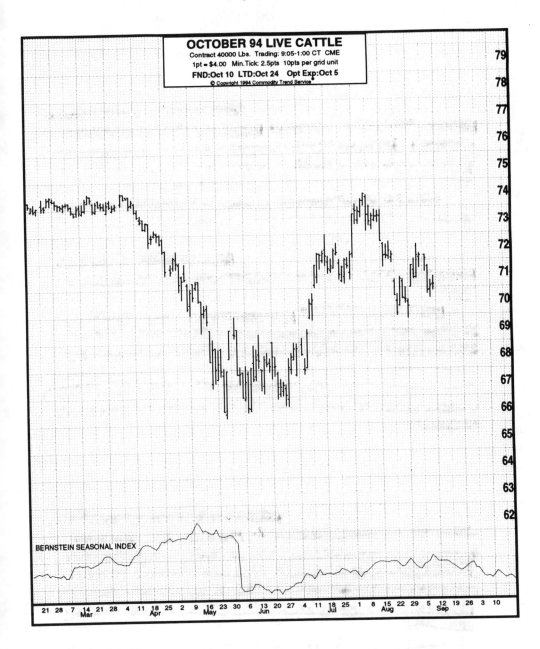

thundering herd has been stopped out, they quietly pick up the pieces and take advantage of the seasonal trade.

For this reason, and because I am determined to discuss only rarely used techniques in this book, I am going to skip any discussion of seasonal trading. But there are many other calendar routines in futures.

Each day has its own routine. Monday, as the opening day, often sets the tone for the week. Tuesday is often a top or bottom of a move. Tuesday at 10:30 A.M is supposedly the favorite time for grain tops and bottoms. It didn't work in grains in 1988 but it sure did work in the stock bottom of 1987.

Wednesday has some of the most powerful trends of the week. If you must daytrade, Wednesday is your day. I believe the big money decides how next week is going to trade on Wednesday and trades accordingly. Thursday is an evening up day as the bigger traders are already maneuvering for the week-end.

Friday is the fear day. In a weather market in grains, if the low of the week is Monday, the high will usually be on Friday. If the high is on Monday, the low of the week will be on Friday. Small traders finally decide to abandon their losing positions as they face a weekend. Gold (and, to a lesser extent, bonds) often is lower on Monday when the world doesn't blow up over the weekend.

Monthly and Quarterly Routines

The month has its routines. The margin on crude oil increases five days before the contract ends. On first notice day of other futures, you can possibly get delivery. As a result, most speculative houses force their clients to roll over or liquidate their contracts at these times. Since the public is mainly long, the end result is artificially low prices. These spot futures normally will rally afterwards.

The floor knows this and usually buys up everything in sight during the period around first notice day (sometimes this doesn't work in extreme bear markets, but Neal Weintraub, who trades on the floor, says 77 percent of the time it does). If floor traders get delivery, they've already made arrangements with their clearing firm or bank to lend the money on the full net worth of the contract. They can borrow $1 million or even $10 million for a day or two on their signature. They only have to pay the interest on that money for the amount of time they are holding the contract.

Another monthly routine is the Social Security effect in cattle. The first weekend after Social Security checks are delivered (usually the third or the fourth day of the month) is a banner day for red meat sales.

Retailers know that consumers will be flush with government checks and monthly payrolls, ready to spend money on high-priced meat. (The end of the month, when people run out of money and can only afford hamburger, is the time for the real grocery sales. Consumers can save at least 5 percent on their grocery bills just by getting all their items then.)

It takes about a week to slaughter cattle, dress the meat, box it, ship it to the cooler of the grocery store, and then have it priced in time for the start of the sales on Thursday. Therefore, a week before Social Security Thursday is a time of higher-than-average cattle prices. A week before the last Thursday of the month is a time of (relatively) low cattle prices.

Many stock traders understand that institutions get new money to invest the first few days of the month and that dividends, monthly salaries and government checks all are issued in the first 10 days of the month. That's why stocks tend to be strong those first 10 days.

Stock traders also know that institutional traders "window dress" before the end of the quarter. If it was a bad quarter for stocks and bonds (like the first quarter of 1994), they will sell stocks and bonds before the last day of the quarter to convince the people whot invest with them that they don't own any losers.

If gold and other commodities did well (just like the first quarter of 1994), they'd buy gold and commodities before the end of the quarter so they can pretend they were smart enough to own the winners. Needless to say, these actions created golden opportunities for those who knew it was time to sell gold and buy stocks and bonds.

Another "Quarterly Routine" is the various government auctions of notes and bonds. By some strange coincidence, the news for bonds and notes always seems to be good just before and just after these auctions.

Invariably any pronounced weakness in the bond and note markets comes at least a week after these auctions, giving government security dealers plenty of time to market or hedge the excess "inventory" they bought during these auctions

The Monthly Brokerage Effect

Here's a dirty little secret that I never could get published in a financial magazine: One of the reasons I wrote this book is to give you the truth, unfiltered and uncensored, about a monthly brokerage effect I call the *End-of-the-Month Commission Rule.*

Brokers are like everyone. They run out of money at the end of the month. When that happens, they become most creative in getting their clients to trade and generate commissions, whether the investment they tout is good for the client or not.

I spent many years as a broker in futures-only firms or as the token futures broker in several stock houses. Believe me, I saw it happen again and again. It's one of the reasons why I quit being a broker. Eventually, I knew I might succumb to this temptation.

In futures, commissions are normally paid monthly based on the entire month's production. In futures, the last day of the month is known as "pay-the-mortgage day." Check out how many times futures make at least a short-term high or low on the last day of the month.

In stocks, it takes five business days from the time a stock is sold until it is settled, i.e., when the money changes hands. Settlement day is the day the broker gets credit for commissions.

See for yourself how many times the stock market has made a short-term high or low five business days from the end of the month.

No, the End-of-the-Month Commission Rule doesn't always work. But if you think the 70-point Dow rally we had on August 24, five business days before the end of the month, didn't have a thing to do with the monthly brokerage effect, you are just like that poor slob in the psych experiment. You refuse to believe what your very eyes tell you because every financial institution is reassuring you it's all an unfortunate coincidence. Coincidences like these are what enables the floor trader to pay for his million-dollar exchange seat.

The Routines of Bull and Bear Markets

One of the most obvious routines is that markets fall faster than they go up. I have seen figures that state, on average, they fall three times faster than they go up. Anyone who saw three years of a bull S&P 500 market disappear in 13 trading days during October 1987 might say that figure is very conservative.

Take some of the other great bull markets in history: the 1973 soybean and cattle market, The 1974 sugar market, the silver market of late 1979 to early 1980. As I pointed out in the first chapter of this book, each collapsed 45 percent in less than two months (just like the 1987 stock market).

Only in sugar did a futures market go up almost as fast as it went down. The average of these four market futures crashes is about 3-to-1—the downside was three times faster than the previous upside move.

This brings me to this major routine of the market: Bear markets make much shallower retracements than bull markets: one-third, one-fifth, and one-eighth retracements versus the .382, .5, .618, etc., retracements of bull markets. It's harder to get back on the train if you attempt to countertrend-trade in a bear market.

There are so many profound trading implications from this

fact I can only begin to scratch the surface of them in this book. Chart patterns that work in bull trends don't work the same in bear markets. A system that is good in an uptrend is not so good in a downtrend. Just like stock trading (with its 50 percent margins) produces different trading patterns than futures trading (with its 5 percent margins), so bear markets must be treated differently than bull markets.

I have not backtested it (I'll leave that to all you out there with those computerized test programs), but I am sure a shorter moving average (like 15 days) works better than a 20-day moving average during down markets. If there is one single reason why there will never be any Holy Grail system that is immensely profitable in all circumstances, the difference between bull and bear markets has got to be it.

Carrying Charges

Another routine that never seems to get the attention it deserves from all those market experts is the carrying charge between different months of the same futures market.

In August of 1994, August Comex gold closed at 383.30 (I'll use this as the cash price of gold). The December gold contract finished at 388.10, a $480 premium over August ($355.10 − $383.30 × 100, the number of ounces in a contract). If gold prices stay level between now and December 1, the price of December gold will gradually fall to 383.30. Since the minimum margin on gold is a little over $1,000, that's about a 45 percent return on your money if you went short and the price of gold held steady.

Today, September Treasury bonds closed at 102–12 while December bonds closed at 101–19, a 25-point ($781) difference (remember that a tick for a bond contract is 1/32). The ratio between the delivery dates of December and September bonds is constant, so for purposes of illustration I will call the September close the cash price. (Yes, I understand that since the September contract is also discounted to the present cash bond price, this figure is not accurate. But for illustration purposes, it will

The minimum margin on one T-bond contract is $2,700. If the cash price of bonds stays the same between now and December and you went long December bonds, that's about a 29 percent return.

Previously I talked about how a 35 percent return would make you rich if you could sustain it over 10 years. Here are 29 percent and 45 percent returns you can have if only gold and bonds remain in nontrending markets—which most markets do 85 percent of the time. It's the futures equivalent of selling an option with a large premium. You get paid to sit.

Here's one way I know to use this premium play in your trading decisions. Whatever future you are thinking about for a premium play, find out the range that occurred before in a time interval equal to the time ahead of your premium future on the day of your analysis.

In the case of gold, December is a little more than three months ahead of when I write. The last three months of trading has seen the closest-to-cash Comex gold contract move in a range of about 20.20, or $2,020 (when you multiply by 100 ounces in a contract), and $480 to $2,020 is about a 23 percent carry charge payout-to-risk ratio. The higher the number, the better the odds to go short (or, in the case of the negative carry charge of bonds, go long).

Of course, markets can suddenly explode against the direction of the carry charge. So this technique, like every technique, cannot be used alone. But it's another thing to consider when your other indicators expect the market to go in the direction of the carrying charge.

Minor (But Profitable) Routines

The *Rule of Doubles* says that when something has doubled in price, it is due for a sell-off. It applies to doubling the money you invested, as well. It's one of the reasons why a floor trader told me to take your money off the table when a future has returned profits equal to the amount you put up in margin. It's also one of the reasons why the Initial-Maintenance Opening Rule works so well.

The *Rule of 72* is usually taken to mean the interest rate rule. If you want to know how long it will take to double your money, divide 72 by the interest percent your money is earning, i.e., your money will double in eight years if you compound it at 9 percent. But futures trading has its own Rule of 72.

If a future has retraced 72 percent of a move, it will (eventually) go all the way back to the start of the move. This rule works better on short-term swings of three days or less.

I'm sure you've seen how a new high or new low will suddenly disappear on your screen as if it never existed. (This is not the obvious bad quote, which is way away from market action.) Wiped-out trades occur because pit conditions are wild and a broker on one side of the pit didn't hear the offer or bid of another broker and went on to the next tick before the other broker had satisfied his offer or bid. It also shows there was not a whole lot of selling (if the wiped-out quote is a high) or buying (if it was a low) at this point. Almost invariably, the market will go back and officially print that wiped-out price.

On the Exchange, quote boards are the yearly high and low of each future traded. When a yearly high or low is taken out, floor traders go with the move. Forget everything you've learned about support and resistance when it comes to taking out the yearly high or low. The floor does over 50 percent of volume on any given day. Their buying or selling power will overwhelm anything in their way.

The importance of these numbers may not seem technically important when a later generation of technicians looks over this action. But the floor knows the truth of the old saying attributed to W. D. Gann: "Trading is learning how to buy high and sell higher; to sell low and buy still lower."

Consider the 1993 bull bond market. For years I used to say at seminars, "Bonds are going to 120." I'd get stares like I was crazy. When an all-time high or low is pierced, you get the yearly high/low effect in spades.

Selling breeds selling and buying breeds buying. If the bond opening is strong, the stock opening will (usually) be strong. If gold is up on the opening, the tendency is for every other commodity from crude oil to soybeans to be up.

It works the same way on the close. If the bonds close on their daily lows, sell the stock market. If the meats are weak, all things being equal (no obvious fundamentals), the grains will close weak.

During the late March/early April period we saw virtually every commodity future rally together and then fall together. We saw every interest rate and stock future do just the opposite. This brings me to the sugar-cattle-copper closing indicator.

When you are a big trader or futures fund, you are like an elephant. Every time you move, you are in danger of smashing something. Your biggest problem (after determining long-term market direction) is to put your orders in in such a way you don't crush the market. So you wait all day, patiently putting in orders little by little. But eventually, there comes the moment of truth—the end of the trading day. If you have anything left to buy or sell, you've got to do it now.

On a normal day, sugar is the first future to close. If it makes a sudden move down or up on the close, it may be a sign that a big boy is making a move. If this pattern continues on the next major futures to close—copper and cattle—look for this pattern to continue in grains, the precious metals, etc.

The Routine of Major Reports

I've discussed how the opening is like a minor report that occurs at regular intervals. It's time now to talk about those dreaded reports like the Producer Price Index, the USDA Pig Crop Report, the July 1st Crop Conditions Report, etc., that can cause drastic changes in markets.

If economic activity were a static affair (or if human emotions didn't come into play), the reaction to reports would go something like this: November soybeans close at 7.00 a bushel before a major crop report. The expectations are for the government to issue an estimate of a two-billion-bushel soybean crop. The market has placed a value on the total crop of $14 billion ($7.00 times two billion). The report comes out and shows a 2.05-billion-bushel soybean crop. Based on this, the opening of November should be 6.83 because 6.83 times 2.05 billion equals $14 billion, the previous amount allocated by the economy to the soybean crop.

We know this is not accurate, because Economics 101 tells us that lower prices will increase demand. So perhaps the November beans should open at 6.90 to reflect this increased demand.

On the other hand, perhaps the estimates put out to the public of a two-billion-bushel crop were simply fodder for the masses. Putting out estimates for a crop report is not a court proceeding. No one is under oath to tell you what he really thinks and nothing *but* what he really thinks.

Even if the firm has customers, the embarrassment of a wrong forecast is nothing compared to the embarrassment of losing in the market. It's possible that everyone was secretly expecting a 2.05-billion-bushel soybean crop but wanted to get as high a price as they could before the report. So perhaps the November beans should really open unchanged or even higher!

The point is that the final arbiter of what a report really means has to be market action, not the chatter of the analysts. Just like the opening, if a market that is expected to open down after a report actually opens unchanged, that is a very powerful buy signal (and vice versa for a bullish report).

New information is constantly entering the market. Many of these reports have been prepared from data collected a long time ago (and much of it may have been leaked to the markets already). Especially when the media have been pounding a certain line (unemployment report expected to pressure bonds), everybody that had to sell or buy (due to emotion or margin calls) will do so before the report. All weak hands have already left the market or changed their position to reflect the obvious way the report will come out. The only traders left daring to go against the media consensus are very strong hands who won't be shaken out even if the report comes out strongly in the direction of the consensus.

In some markets, like the bond market, there seems to be a report that moves the market every day. On some days there are many reports in the bond market (7:30 A.M. and 9:00 A.M. government reports, a report from a Federal Reserve bank, or auction results). But there are two basic market formations that occur before major reports that either your broker or the media will be talking about as "biggies":

1. **Weak Hands Formation.** A few days before a major report, the market will temporarily bottom or top, usually at some minor support or resistance area obvious on the chart. Then there is a small countertrend rally right up to the time the report is issued as weak hands are frightened out of the market. Most of the time the report confirms the trend and the market goes on to make new lows or highs.

2. **Panic Formation.** In this case, the market hammers down into a major support level or rockets up to a major resistance level just before the report is issued. After the report is issued, the market has a major reversal even if the report is even worse than the market expected, forcing a new high or low on the opening after the report.

Figure 6-2, A shows the June bonds during late March and early April. A is the day before and the day of the infamous March 1994 Unemployment Report issued April 1, 1994. It was infamous not only for the bond collapse that followed but also for its release on Good Friday (this may have been the only time in history the U.S. markets have traded on this holiday).

Since the next Monday was an Easter Monday holiday in Europe, the American traders had two days to themselves to trade the U.S. bond market without major competition. Being unable to take protection or advantage of a major report without skipping your vacation and trading long distance for two days would have been enough to shake the strongest European trader.

Since the trend had been strongly down, it must have been irresistible for these traders to take their profits by buying in their short contracts. This alone should have tipped everyone off that the report was going to be bearish.

But the action before the report was also a classic example of the weak hands formation. Long bonds attempted to bottom at the 7 1/8 percent and 7 3/16 percent yield area two days before the report. There was even a 38-point ($1,250) one-day rally before the report came out that probably frightened a lot of small-time shorts.

Figure 6–2, B is a good illustration of the panic formation before a report. The bond market has been in a major downtrend for four months. Before the report was released, virtually nobody had made any money being long in logn bonds. The media was singing a dirge, warning traders about how the May 12, 1994, triple-threat release of the weekly unemployment numbers, re-tail sales, and the Producer Price Index was going to drive bonds to the floor.

But the market was right at a major support level—a sup-port level, however, that was virtually unknown to the average trader. The 1981 all-time high in 30-year bond yields was 15.17 percent. The 1993 yield low was 5.77 percent. A 20 percent, one-fifth retracement of this move was 7.65 percent yield. The market had been bouncing off this level for four days before the report, including the time right before the report. A classic panic formation.

First through the Even

About a decade age I had the privilege of working with "Sandy," the stock market specialist I spoke about previously. Sandy told me how his fellow specialists borrowed millions from the Fed at below-market rates like 4 percent (that was the days of double-digit interest rates), how they used inside chart days on the Dow as a special code among themselves to tell where the stock market was going, and the importance of the two-step top in stocks (we

Figure 6–2

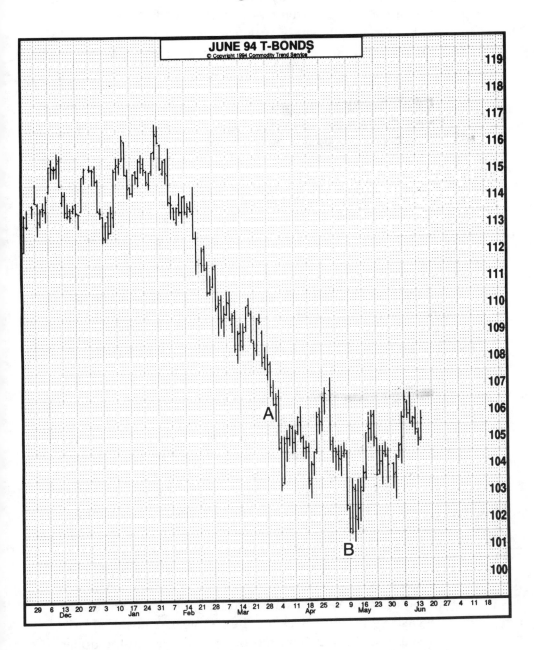

JUNE 94 T-BONDS
© Copyright 1994 Commodity Trend Service

ught be going through this process now). But by far the most profitable advice he gave me was *First through the Even*.

In January 1980, Sandy was approached by a large floor trader making millions of paper profits from thousands of long gold contracts. Understandably nervous, the local asked Sandy "When do I cash in my longs?"

"First through the Even," replied Sandy.

There is a natural tendency for investors to take profits at even numbers—$9.00 silver, $8.00 soybeans, etc. The first time a market goes through these even numbers, up or down, normally there is a counterreaction. At that time in 1980, the big gold contracts were the June IMM and Comex gold contracts. Sandy told the gold floor trader to sell when June gold traded over $900. Even if this wasn't *the* top, the natural sell-off that followed would give the floor trader a chance to get back on board if he thought the market was going higher. Actually, the floor trader sold at the historical high point of gold. In gratitude, he gave Sandy a commission of 1 percent of the difference between where he sold and where he would have likely sold if he hadn't gotten Sandy's advice. That 1 percent commission was $250,000!

There is a four-step process in First through the Even:

1. **The Approach**—the lead future approaches an even number but reverses just before touching it. This approach number is fairly predictable (like 6.95 or 101 yen to the dollar). In fact, among the major futures, the market often bounces off the approach number several times.

    There is a tendency for the biggest futures, what I call Level 1 futures, to bounce off an approach number three times before an actual First through the Even happens. A classic example was how the Dow bounced three times off 1,000 (January 1966, November 1968, September 1972) before finally overcoming the 1,000 barrier. Another example is contained in Figure 6–3, which has the cash yen daily prices for the last year. You can clearly see that the yen bounced off the 101 yen-to-the-dollar cross-rate three times (examples A, B, C).

    Level 1 futures would be the trillion-dollar futures

like gold, crude oil, major currencies, bonds, and Euro-dollars. Level 2 is the next stop down—major agricultural futures like soybeans, sugar, and cattle, and silver, copper, etc. Level 3 would be the minor contracts like orange juice and lumber.

Level 2 futures usually bounce twice off the approach number before going to a First through the Even. In Figure 6–4, March corn (which was the closest-to-cash future at the time) bounced twice (examples A and B) off 2.99 before finally going past and closing above 3.00 on December 27 (C).

Level 3 futures bounce once off the approach number. Figure 6–5 shows how the orange juice market bounced off the 1.00 level in October 1993 (A) before going through the 1.00 price (B).

2. **The Touch**—The future or cash index touches the even number, reverses for a very short time, and then quickly surges beyond it. Normally, only floor traders can take advantage of this move.

3. **First through the Even**—The future or cash index goes sightly beyond the even number and then reverses back to the approach number.

4. **First Close through the Even**—The first close above or below an even number is often the top or bottom of a move. Classically, this close is immediately followed by a long-term reversal.

The reason I mentioned cash indexes is that often the four-step dance of First through the Even happens twice—once for the future, and once for the cash.

Figure 6–6 has the last two weeks of May 1994 in the May, Soybean futures. On May 18 the May future closed over 7.00 (A)—the first time bean futures had closed over 7.00 in months, creating a First Close through the Even. On May 20, the July soybean future, now the spot month, fell back toward the natural approach number of 6.95 (Figure 6–7, A).

Figure 6-3

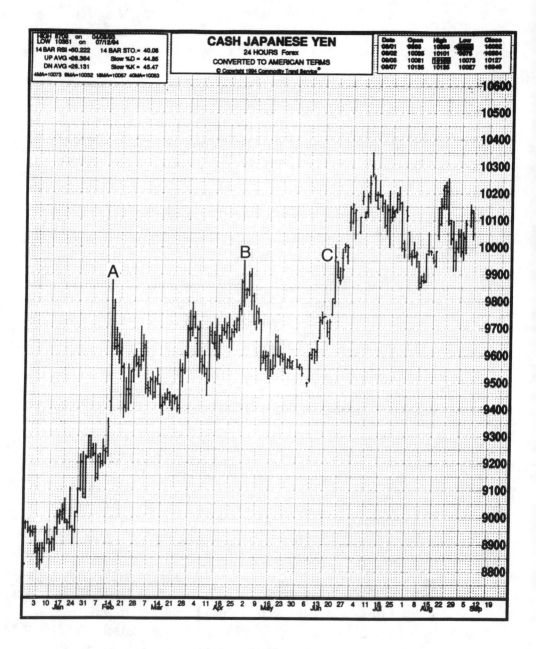

Figure 6-4

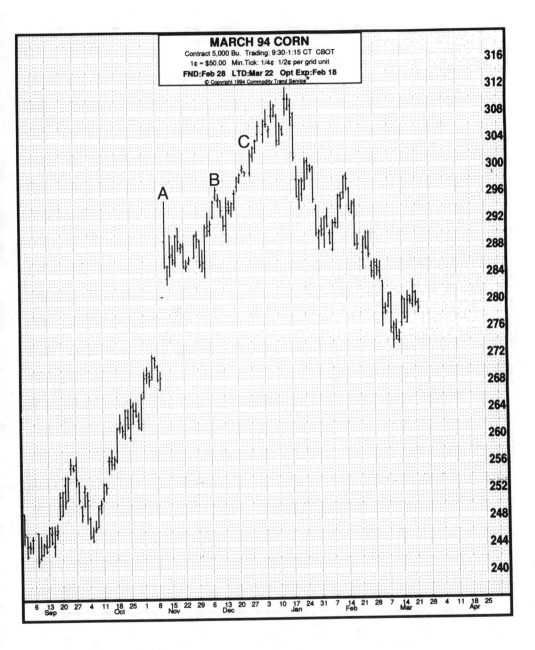

MARCH 94 CORN
Contract 5,000 Bu. Trading: 9:30-1:15 CT CBOT
1¢ = $50.00 Min.Tick: 1/4¢ 1/2¢ per grid unit
FND:Feb 28 LTD:Mar 22 Opt Exp:Feb 18
© Copyright 1994 Commodity Trend Service

Figure 6–5

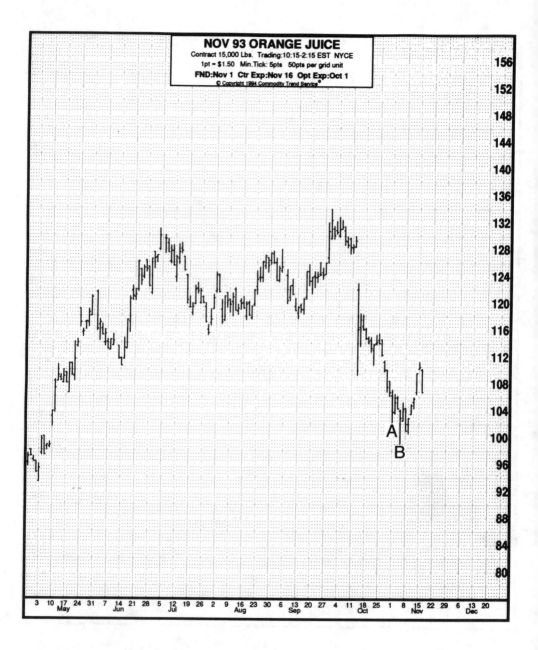

NOV 93 ORANGE JUICE
Contract 15,000 Lbs. Trading:10:15-2:15 EST NYCE
1pt = $1.50 Min.Tick: 5pts 50pts per grid unit
FND:Nov 1 Ctr Exp:Nov 16 Opt Exp:Oct 1
© Copyright 1994 Commodity Trend Service

Finally, cash beans (as recorded in *The Wall Street Journal*) closed above 7.00 for the first time in almost a year. It was no accident that this was the top of the great grain bull of 1994. In 1988, the top of the bean market occurred when the cash market finally closed over 10.00 a bushel. Again and again, a First Close through the Even has been the tops and bottoms of many markets.

This trading rule works on interest rates and currencies, but you must substitute yields (like 7 1/4 percent) and cross-rates for futures prices.

In late June, the Japanese yen finally burst the 100 yen barrier (Figure 6–8, A). By a happy accident of mathematics, that also was the same as 100 in the future. On June 21, the September yen closed above 100, at 100.65, and then promptly fell back a little past the 101 yen/dollar cross-rate approach number, or 98.70 in the futures (B).

Remember the panic formation example above in bonds? The lowest cash close was on May 9 (7.63 percent). It was a classic First Close through the Even based on 7 5/8 yield (7.62 percent).

When First through the Even fails (or a First Close through the Even), it almost always is a signal of a long-term top, or three-week topping period. After bouncing off the approach number, the September yen went back over 100 and the 100 yen/dollar cross-rate three days after a First Close through the Even. This was a signal that a long-term top was forming in the yen (Figure 6–8, C).

The first time the September yen went over 100, it was for approximately three hours. Using the Rule of Three, when the yen futures stayed over 100 for three days in a row, it suggested that the next top would be made approximately a three-week movement away from 100.

Since the September yen was moving about four basis points a week, that would suggest a possible top around 104 in futures, or a 96 yen/dollar cross-rate. The 96 yen/dollar cross-rate also was an ideal approach number for 95, the next logical First through the Even number for Japanese yen (Figure 6–8, D).

Figure 6–6

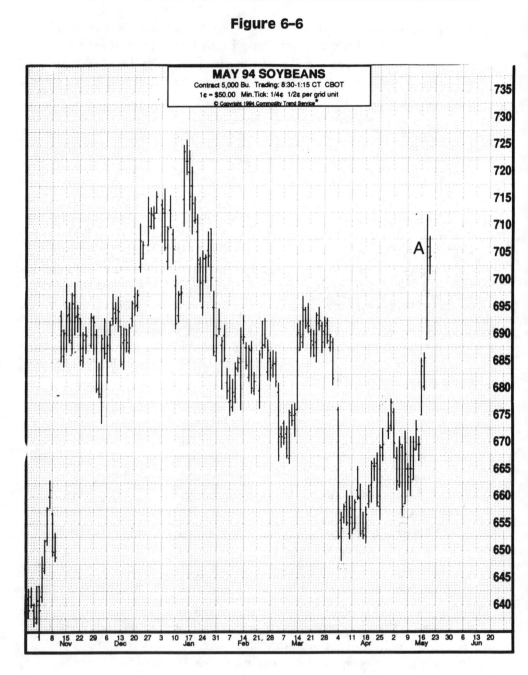

MAY 94 SOYBEANS
Contract 5,000 Bu. Trading: 8:30-1:15 CT CBOT
1¢ = $50.00 Min.Tick: 1/4¢ 1/2¢ per grid unit
© Copyright 1994 Commodity Trend Service®

Figure 6–7

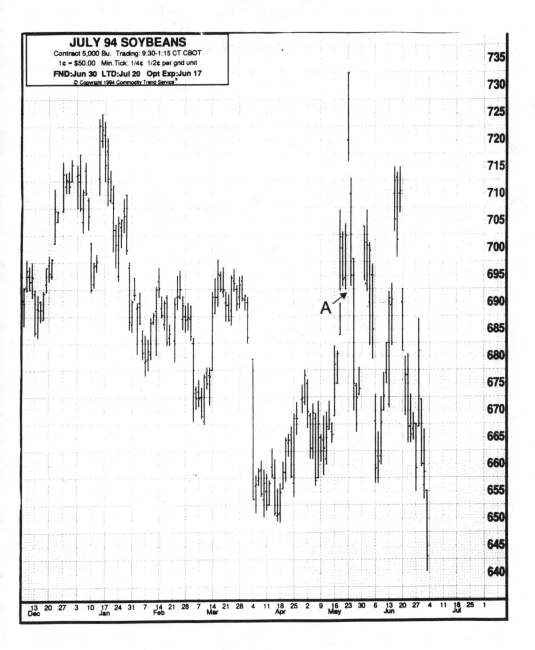

JULY 94 SOYBEANS
Contract 5,000 Bu. Trading: 9:30-1:15 CT CBOT
1¢ = $50.00 Min.Tick: 1/4¢ 1/2¢ per grid unit
FND:Jun 30 LTD:Jul 20 Opt Exp:Jun 17
© Copyright 1994 Commodity Trend Service

Writing this in late August 1994, I don't know if this is the ultimate top for the Japanese yen versus the dollar. If the Clinton administration is a replay of the Carter administration, it's possible that just like the Swiss franc (the leading speculative currency of the time) topped out for nine years in the summer of 1978, the yen may have topped for a some time.

The media hysteria at the time (more on this in a later chapter), and First through the Even suggest the recent top in yen is going to last long enough for all of us to make a lot of money going short yen.

This indicator works better in bull markets than bear markets. The chance to take profits around even numbers is overpowering among the happy public bulls. Since professionals are the usual shorts in bear markets, this "take-profits-now-that-we-are-here" impulse is muted when an even number is breached on the downside. But even in bear markets, I would still watch for the four steps of First through the Even. It may not make you $25 million like that gold floor trader, but it will pay off your if you watch this indicator many times over.

Figure 6–8

CASH JAPANESE YEN
24 HOURS Forex
© Copyright 1994 Commodity Trend Service
CONVERTED TO AMERICAN TERMS

Chapter Seven

Expected Range

This is a chapter I almost didn't write. But if I am honestly going to examine some of the main methods floor traders use, I have to do it.

There are many, many telephone services and seminars that cater to the daytrade market and, for a fee, will tell you what they expect tomorrow's range will be in various futures—or at least how to calculate it. There are three things you need to keep in mind when you see ads for this type of service and seminar:

1. Every system is subject to the Mathematics of Investing. If you are going to daytrade, come to Chicago, join the MidAm, and do things right. Yes, you might beat the odds for a while, but if you are really that good of a short-term trader, you'd be much better off coming to the center of the futures universe and renting or owning some sort of exchange seat. Every time I have listened to or read something about great futures traders, there is at least one point that comes through loud and clear. They love what they are doing. Even the drudgery is no drudgery to them. They love to study, calculate, and talk about the markets during the long hours when there is really nothing specific to do. (Learning to wait for the

right time to trade is half the battle.) If you really love something or someone, you want to be around them all the time. If you really love trading—not the money and excitement you think it will bring—you won't balk at making the sacrifices necessary to become a good trader. There are many great traders (perhaps most of them) who trade away from the floor. But:

* Most of them depend on trading methods other than daytrading.

* If they do daytrade, they operate with rock-bottom commissions and a thorough knowledge of the floor because many of them started as floor traders.

* They started daytrading in a time that was much more forgiving for mistakes if you did daytrade and now know what to do.

Let me try to explain this third point. From 1973 to 1984, T-bill rates averaged in the double-digit range. If you had $100,000 in your futures account and got a 10 percent T-bill interest rate on your money, that gave you $10,000 for losses, equipment charges, etc. The Mathematics of Investing were a little more in your favor. In addition, we continuously had wild swings in almost every futures market. Many markets, like the S&P 500, were just starting. As a result, they were loaded with opportunities for the astute trader as novice traders and their money rolled in. Finally, not everybody was computerized in those days, i.e., knowing about stochastics might have given you a real advantage then, not like today.

2. Market conditions change every morning. The opening price has already shattered that comfortable technical world your 900-number or sure-thing range finder generated the night before.

3. The range of many, if not most, trading days is more of an accident than you might think.

While floor traders do over 50 percent of the volume, most of the market-making moves are made by the big institutions. If they are not in the market in a big way, there can be a lot of meaningless churning. Highs and lows get made simply because the floor found going one way or the other was not generating outside orders and quit. Floor traders were simply cutting each other up, so they stepped aside at some point or even got off the floor. This happens not just on slow days, before holidays, or when a snowstorm hits the market. (Volume studies are a good way to see if that was a nothing day. One way to measure volume is the resistance index. The resistance index is the number of contracts traded in a future divided by the sum created by subtracting the low from the high.)

So a word to the wise. If your range-finding service or method treats every previous day alike in making its calculations of tomorrow's range, if it doesn't adjust for today's opening, you may find yourself in difficulty.

Rather than a panacea for daytrading, most traders should use any method that generates an expected range for that day's trading as a starting point for their market entry system. By a market entry system, I mean a method that will help you put your buy order nearer the bottom of the day and your sell orders near the top of the day than mere chance would dictate. Unlike the average floor trader, you are not looking to get out before the end of the day unless prices have moved against you. You are not daytrading. You are simply making a decision: "I probably want to buy or sell today if XYZ happens. If that happens, I am going to use market entry techniques to minimize my exposure."

The Pivot

Computers are banned on the pits of most exchanges. In any case, it would be very difficult to look at a screen in one hand and try to trade with the other. Floor traders have had to develop simple range-finding systems that they can keep in their head or on the back of their trading card. The most common expected-range system floor traders have used in the past is the "Pivot."

First, you calculate the pivot point (sometimes called the

daily average), which is merely the sum of the high, low, and close of a future divided by 3. (For illustration purposes only, I'm going to use artificially simple numbers.) If the high was 10, the low 6, and the close 7, the pivot point would be 7.67 (or 23 divided by 3). After we have found the pivot point, we compute the next high and the next low. The next high equals the pivot point times 2 minus the low, or 9.34 ($7.67 \times 2 = 15.34 - 6 = 9.34$). The next low is the pivot point times 2 (which we have already calculated as 15.34) minus the high of 10, or 5.34. The next points to compute are the highest high and the lowest low.

The highest high is the pivot point (7.67) minus the next low (5.34) plus the next high (9.34), or 11.67 ($7.67 - 5.34 + 9.34 = 11.67$). The lowest low is the pivot point (7.67) minus the sum of the next high minus the next low ($9.34 - 5.34 = 4.00$), or 3.67 ($7.67 - 4$).

In review:

1. Pivot point = previous day's high + low + close divided by 3.

2. Next high = 2 × pivot point minus the low.

3. Next low = 2 × pivot point minus the high.

4. Highest high = pivot point minus next low plus next high.

5. Lowest low = pivot point minus the sum of the next high minus the next low.

The pivot point, or Pivot, is the average. Above it you are bullish. Below it you are bearish. If the market is in an uptrend and you are above the Pivot, you buy. If the market is in a downtrend and you are below the Pivot, you sell. If the market is neutral, you use the next high to sell against and the lowest low to buy against. (The public uses the next low to do its favorite thing: buy the market. This number usually doesn't hold as a support level.)

These rules are not set in stone. The key to all range trading is resonation. The more reasons (such as First through the Even, the Rule of Three, the Rule of Doubles, etc.) you can find that predict the same number (resonate), the more likely the market will stall at that number and give you a logical spot to buy or sell.

One variation of the Pivot is to add today's opening to yesterday's high, low, and close and divide that sum by 4 to give you a pivot point. Another would be to substitute today's opening for yesterday's close. You simply add the opening to the sum of yesterday's high and low and divide this total by three to get your Pivot.

I have not done an exhaustive computer study on the question of whether to use the opening or the close to calculate the Pivot. My suggestion based on some preliminary work is to use the traditional Pivot to determine support and resistance on the opening. Then, a few minutes after the opening, substitute the opening for the close in creating a new Pivot. In hectic markets it may take a minute or two to establish the exact prices of the 30-second opening range. Then it will take another minute or two for the clerks of the floor traders to do the calculations and send the new open Pivot into the pit. Then it might be another minute or two before the floor trader can actually look down to see the new numbers in the hectic conditions of the opening trades.

Remember, even though many of these floor traders are like human computers, making all these calculations in your head at the most critical time of day is risky. The floor trader knows much of his potential trading profit for the whole day hangs on how well he does in the opening. The best most of them can manage is to memorize the numbers generated from the close Pivot and wait until their clerk tells them the new open Pivot numbers.

The secret of the Pivot system is the same secret of any logical trading strategy. It's elementary physics: A body that is in motion will stay in motion in the same direction until it meets resistance equal to or greater than its velocity. The Pivot is just a numeric representation of where the average trader bought or sold yesterday. If the average seller of yesterday is losing, there will be a tendency for him to cover and send prices higher. If the average buyer of yesterday is losing, he will likely sell and send prices still lower. At some point in the day, prices will attempt to stabilize, if for no other reason than profit-taking and the desire of floor traders to even up their positions before the close. The highest high and lowest low are an attempt to find out the approximate area where that might happen.

The Four Quadrants

There's another relatively simple way to find an expected range for today's trading. I call it the *Four Quadrants*.

Take three moving averages of varying length. I used exponential moving averages of the last 5, 21, and 55 days of openings when I tested it. But today I don't believe it's that important what type of moving average you use (simple, weighted, exponential, displaced, etc.), or the exact numbers you use for your moving averages (I prefer using openings to closes for trading a few minutes after the opening). The key is to make sure you use at least three moving averages that are space somewhat apart. If you are using a simple 18-day moving average already, you can simply add in a small moving average (say three to five days) and a larger one (say 40–60 days).

Let's say the five-ay moving average of future X is 100 while the 20-day and 60-day moving averages are 95 and 90 respectively. Yesterday's close in X was 96. The four quadrants are placed along a line; quadrant 1 is above the highest moving average (in this case above 100); quadrant 2 is between the highest and the second highest moving average (100 and 95 in this example); quadrant 3 is between the second highest and the lowest moving average (95 and 90); and quadrant 4 is below the lowest moving average (in this example, the area below 90).

The wider the range between the highest and lowest moving average, the more that future is trending. When the shortest and middle average converge, a short-term trend change is imminent. When all three moving averages converge, a long-term trend change is imminent.

To generate an expected range for today's action, you find the closest moving averages that are within a limit move of the future. For the purpose of our very hypothetical example, let's assume a limit move is three full points (i.e., our future has a maximum range of 99 on the upside and 93 on the downside). In this case, only one moving average is within a limit move of the close of future X: the 20-day moving average of 95.

Next we take this moving average, 95, and compare it with the next lowest moving average, which is the 60-day moving average at 90. We add both of those numbers together and divide by two to get a midpoint number of 92.5. Since this number is out of range for today, we take that midpoint number (92.5) and the original average that was in range (95) and add them together and divide that number by two to get 93.75. That number is in range and becomes our second support number (95 is our first support number). To get our resistance number, we go through the same procedure with the moving average that is in range (the 20-day at 95) and the next highest future (the five-day at 100).

In big trends, sometimes there is no moving average in range, or only the top or bottom moving average is in range (of a limit move). In that case we use a flip to generate a hypothetical moving average to generate our support and resistance numbers.

Let's use the same moving average above but change the close of future X to 104. A limit move is 101, which is out of range for the highest moving average. The difference between the highest moving average (the five-day at 100) and the second highest (the 20-day at 95) is five. We "flip" this number by adding it to the highest moving average (the five-day at 100) to create a new artificial moving average at 105. Then we go through the same calculations as before to determine our support number (102.5). 105 now becomes our new resistance number. We can divide again to create a second support number at 103.75 and a second resistance number at 106.25. (You do this until you have at least two support and two resistance points within the limit move of the future up or down).

I claim nothing for these numbers other than they work as well as trend lines, Bollinger Bands, and other more common techniques of determining support and resistance. Their only weakness is the relatively rare event when all three moving averages get so close together there isn't much space to create support and resistance points. At this point you may have to do several flips to get numbers that correspond to the range where the future has been trading for the last few weeks or days.

I'll leave it to those with the megadrives to find the optimum set of three averages for each future. I like the Four Quadrant Method more than other support and resistance techniques because:

1. It is simple—you only need a spreadsheet or a calculator, not any special software like Bollinger Bands, etc.

2. You get two indicators in one. You get support/resistance plus the added insight of a Moving Average Convergence/Divergence (MACD).

3. The movement of the future among the four quadrants can give you a graphic insight into what is happening with that future, an insight no black-box software program can give.

You remember "Sandy," who taught me about First through the Even? He did all his calculations by hand because he coud "see" more things that way. There are many, many first-class traders that believe the same thing.

Before you sneer, let me say one thing. I've seen a lot more successful traders doing calculations by hand than I have black-box daytraders with all their fancy permutations of the Sacred Six.

Chapter Eight

Fib Times

The physical world is measured in three dimensions: height, width, and depth. The floor trader's world also has three dimensions: the opening, which tells him how high or low he can expect the market to move, the routine of the market, which shows him how deep (in terms of volume and risk) he can trade, and the expected range, or what to expect for the width of today's move.

According to Einstein, time is the fourth physical dimension. But this fourth dimension can only be observed on earth by careful observation during special circumstances. Time is also the fourth dimension of the floor trading world. When you first look at it, it seems to be only a routine. But after careful observation, you realize it is more than just a normal routine. It's so important to the floor trader it deserves a chapter of its own.

In a backhanded way, I've talked about the routine of time throughout the first chapters of this book: the 10:20–10:40 A.M. Fed time in bonds, Tuesday at 10:30 A.M. as a potential topping time, how the strength (or weakness) of openings or closes of one future might influence another, how floor traders come up after the opening to take a break until the New York lunch hour or the noon balloon in ag contracts.

There are other minor time routines:

1. Meats often make highs and lows just before the opening of the grains. The price of grain is such a huge component of meat prices, often it seems you are trading the direction of grains as much as that of hogs and cattle (much like the relationship between stocks and bonds).This unknown factor reaches its peak of greed or fear in the heart of the average public meat trader just before grains open. And like most ag futures, the meats have more small traders than average.

2. London markets usually close around 10:00 A.M. London trades more deutsche marks than Chicago and New York combined. It is the dominant world market, the primary market for currencies, gold, platinum, copper, cocoa, sugar, and crude oil. (Don't be fooled by the fact that New York trades more crude oil contracts than London. Brent is still the standard of the world, thanks to its proximity to the Middle East. Brent going over $40—a First through the Even—was the top of the 1990 bull market in crude oil.)

After London closes in those markets it dominates, U.S. traders usually do one of two things. If things were dull in London, they'll be duller in the U.S., so U.S. floor traders start drifting off the floor. But if a London-dominated market had lots of excitement, U.S. floor traders and commercials have a chance to go wild without the interference of London arbitrageurs. Just like London often makes extreme quotes in U.S. bonds before the main U.S. trading begins, U.S. markets often make extreme quotes in London-dominated markets after 10:00 A.M.

The advent of 24-hour trading has made the element of time a harder thing to apply in trading. The idea of an opening price is getting strained (although, as I pointed out before, not lost). Around-the-clock trading has the opposite effect of a snowstorm in New York or Chicago. In a snowstorm, traders try to get everything done in a few hours so they can go home early (whether or not the exchange officially closes early). With 24-hour trading, volume fades in and out, making it difficult to determine just what is a significant time in trading. Both throw off the time routine of the day.

In analyzing how to use time, you have to do the same thing as you would for any other aspect of trading some future. You have to determine the primary market. If it is London, you are going to have to look at the same charts and fundamentals that London is looking at. If you want to trade rice (and possibly the yen), you should attempt to understand how the Japanese trade that market.

The big money is made in the big markets by big players through big moves. Rotterdam may make a new high in soybean meal, but if it is not validated by Chicago, the big money won't follow it. On March 2, 1994, the London market in U.S. bonds collapsed along with all the other European bond markets. But after a sell-off about half the size of London's, U.S. bonds rallied several days before going lower than the London low the following week. The London move was premature.

Market wizard and megacurrency trader Bruce Kovner says he has assistants that can help him trade through the night. Totally absorbed in his work, he sometimes trades all night if market conditions warrant it.

For the rest of us mere mortals, I have a suggestion—especially if the size of your account demands any trading in half-size MidAm contracts that don't trade all night. Use the London closing time of 10:00 A.M. as your close and trade accordingly. If you have enough money to trade full contracts of London-dominated futures, and if they have enough volume for your type of trading during London's opening hours on Globex or some other night trading system, then use London's hours for any time routine and be prepared to get up very, very early in the morning to catch London's all-important opening.

For all the above reasons and because watching the U.S. media doesn't work as well on London-dominated futures, I recommend novice traders stick to U.S.-dominated futures. The "Fib Times" I am giving are only for the trading hours of U.S.

markets. Even though I am going to give them for London-dominated markets, I recommend you use them with large grains of salt in these markets.

I first learned about Fib Times from a floor trader. He called it "the eighths." He divided up the trading day into eight equal parts. He insisted the market made intraday highs and lows at these eighths: the 1/8 time, 1/4 time, the 3/8 time, etc. After investigating it, I found out he was right. These time points in the trading day were experiencing intraday highs and lows far beyond what you would expect from chance.

Then I got the bright idea if the one-eighth times were working, what about dividing the day's range by other Fibonnaci numbers (3, 5, 13, .382, .618, etc.)? They worked as well. I called them Fib Points (of time) at first. But that name only confused technicians who used the same name for certain chart points. So now I call them Fib Times to prevent confusion.

To determine Fib Times, you first determine the amount of minutes a market trades. For example, crude oil trades 325 minutes a day from (8:45 A.M. to 2:10 P.M.). 325 divided by 13 gives a 25-minute interval for the 1/13th Fib Time. The first 1/13th would be 25 minutes after the opening at 9:10 A.M. The next would be at 9:35 A.M., the next at 10 A.M., etc.

A crude oil floor trader would use Fib Times in the following way. He's observed that crude has a downward bias. At 9:10 A.M. he sees that the market has moved up to a resistance point, which he could determine either by market orders at that point or by some other sort of analysis. Now he has both time and price confirming his trade.

These two factors also confirm his exit strategy. He can use a price stop to get out if he loses and a price objective if he wins. He can also use some Fib Time to get out even if his price stop or objective hasn't been reached. He may decide that if he doesn't make 10 points by the next Fib Time at 9:35, he's getting out. The trader now has three indicators working for him: direction (the downward bias), price (resistance), and time (the 9:10 A.M. crude oil Fib Time).

Table 8-1 shows the most prominent Fib Times:

Table 8-1

Fib Time	Gold	Interest Currency	Copper	Stock (Futures)	Crude Oil	Sugar	Cattle	Grains
1/13	7:48A.M.	7:51A.M.	8:46A.M.	9:01A.M	9:10A.M	9:17A.M.	9:18A.M.	9:47A.M.
1/8	8:06	8:10	8:59	9:21	9:26	9:28	9:34	9:58
1/5	8:34	8:40	9:20	9:51	9:50	9:45	9:47	10:15
2/8	8:52	9:00	9:34	10:11	10:07	9:56	10:04	10:24
1/3	9:23	9:33	9:57	10:45	10:33	10:15	10:23	10:45
.382	9:41	9:53	10:10	11:05	10:49	10:25	10:30	10:56
4/8	10:25	10:40	10:43	11:53	11:29	10:52	11:03	11:22
.618	11:09	11:27	11:15	12:40P.M.	12:06P.M.	11:18	11:25	11:49
2/3	11:27	11:47	11:28	1:00	12:22	11:30	11:42	12:00P.M.
6/8	12:02P.M.	12:20P.M.	11:52	1:35	12:49	11:48	12:01P.M.	12:19
4/5	12:16	12:40	12:05P.M.	1:54	1:05	11:58	12:13	12:30
7/8	12:43	1:10	12:26	2:26	1:30	12:16P.M.	12:30	12:47
12/13	1:02	1:29	12:39	2:44	1:45	12:26	12:42	12:58

There are obvious problems with this table. I didn't want to put down all the 1/13ths and other Fib Times, although in futures like bonds, crude, and stocks that have long trading sessions, they have some significance. Nor did I want to calculate all the night sessions and 24-hour trading Fib Times.

I am going to leave the previous two calculations to you for reasons of space and simplicity. It's bad enough the exchanges have recently played around with the opening times of grains and livestock. This chart is bound to become obsolete some time in the future. I'm afraid you are constantly going to have to be on the lookout to see if you must recalculate these times.

I'm sure some are thinking, "This is like Gann or some other esoteric charting technique. You've got so many points, you are bound to hit a high or low. How can you tell which point will be significant on a given day?" There are three basic steps:

Step One: Match the Fib Times
with Other Routines

If you are trading bonds, compare the Fib Times based on the time range of only the day session with the Fib Times of the entire trading day including the night session. Where these Fib Times intersect are points of time likely to have intraday tops and bottoms. You could do the same Fib Time comparisons between London and the equivalent U.S. future in London-dominated markets.

The 2/13th Fib Time in cattle is 9:31 A.M., right at the grain opening. The 4/8ths Fib Time in bonds is 10:40 A.M., near the time the Federal Reserve jiggles the money supply. A prominent Fib Time for stocks and bonds is 9:00 A.M., the time the government issues reports.

It's very common for expected events that have no specific time (like an earnings report for IBM, a Treasury auction result, or a Federal Reserve announcement) to come at Fib Times. The more routines you can find out about, the better you will understand what Fib Time will be significant for that trading day.

Step Two: Determine the Underlying
Trend of a Market

Is it bullish, bearish, or a trading range? Is it a volatile market full of news or a quiet market waiting for some sort of news to move it? Slow markets or markets anticipating a report usually have the most movement at either the opening 1/13 or the closing 12/13 Fib Time.

In bear markets, typical periods of strength come after the opening 1/13 until the appropriate public lunch hour—New York's lunch hour (11:10 to 11:50 A.M.) or the noon balloon of U.S. agricultural futures. This is the time you want to sell to get in on the trend and the collapse on the close.

In bull markets, it's just the opposite. After the initial opening 1/13 surge, the market typically fades back to the previous close until reaching a bottom around the appropriate lunch hour. Then it rallies until the close.

Step Three: Is Your Market a Leader or a Follower?

All U.S. futures in London-dominated markets are followers, but this also can occur in U.S. primary markets. Sometimes gold is the leader (like 1979–1980). Sometimes it's the Dollar that every other future is keying off of. At these times, it's important to keep in mind conjunctions of Fib Times.

In the fall of 1990 the skyrocketing price of crude was on the minds of everyone. If Saddam Hussein blew up Saudi Arabia, the price of oil could go sky high, causing stocks and bonds to collapse. Every S&P 500 trader was keeping one eye on the price of crude, and it shows in the interday charts. Often a crude oil Fib Time was the top or bottom of the intraday Dow chart. The conjunction of the 2/8 Fib Time for crude at 10:07 and the 2/8 Fib Time of stocks at 10:11 often was the time of peaks and bottoms in the Dow.

Fib Times can also be used to determine stops. The Rule of 72 also applies to time. A future that makes a new high or low after 72 percent of the day's trading is completed will usually not reverse itself later in the day. Witness the following quote from the July 1990 issue of *Stocks & Commodities* magazine:

> Every day at 1:00 P.M. we check the 12:00–1:00 P.M. hourly bar of the T-bond contract. If the tick volume (the number of times the future has moved one tick up or down) is greater than 100, we then place two orders—a buy-stop one tick above the high of the bar and a sell-stop one tick below the low of the bar.
>
> If either order is filled before 2:00 P.M., we cancel the other and place a $1,500 money management stop-loss. We then do nothing until 1:00 P.M. when we again look at the 12:00–1:00 P.M. bar. If we are long and not stopped out and today's 1:00 P.M. bar tick volume is greater than 100, we would place a sell order for two contracts one tick below the low of the bar.
>
> If we are filled to the short side before 2:00 P.M. we would then use a new $1,500 stop. If we are not filled,

we cancel the sell-stop below the 1:00 P.M. bar and reinstate our original $1,500 money management sell-stop. We again have nothing to do until the next day at 1:00 P.M.

The author, Charles Wright, claimed this system earned 476 percent through the first 10 months of 1989. Whether this was exactly true or whether this system continues to work as well now, I don't know. But it is typical of the evidence I have seen of the power of the Rule of 72.

The trend is definitely your friend in the latter stages of the day. The public stubbornly carries losses until the last minute, hoping for a miracle reversal. The funds also like to use ham-fisted, close-only orders to make sure of the trend. The pros have long since positioned themselves for the close.

Another rule is never take a losing position into the last 1/13th. It's a very rare day when the market has a strong reversal during the last 1/13th. When it does happens, it is almost invariably a sign of a major top or bottom.

Key reversals often start after the opening 1/13th, especially after reports. The Tuesday at 10:30 A.M rule for grain tops or bottoms reflects the 2/8th (10:24 A.M.) and 1/3rd Fib Time (10:37). By that time, professional traders figure that enough weak hands have been squeezed out of the market, and they begin the long trek to the close accumulating positions.

Like expected range, I almost hate to put out this information on Fib Times. Invariably, people will take these concepts and try to make them into a daytrade system, completely ignoring the Mathematics of Investing. I've seen brokers become completely oblivious to everything else once I've told them about Fib Times. They watch the screen, fascinated, exclaiming, "There's another Fib Time reversal. And another one!" Unfortunately, most Fib Times can only be used by floor traders, they of the $1.00 commission.

I prefer people use Fib Times as an adjunct to their own longer-term systems. It's another way to help you sell the upper quadrant or buy the lower quadrant of price action when you have determined that today is the day you would like to enter a market. Shaving off a few hundred this week here and a few hundred the next week there off the cost of your fills are those nickels that turn into millions.

A stock market that loses 20 percent in an hour (as in 1987) or a soybean market that collapses 5 percent in a matter of minutes (as in 1988) can completely overwhelm any price-only based system of entry dependent on protective stops (Neal Weintraub claims he has seen currency stops filled over 100 points away from their trigger price). Without the element of what time it is in your trading, even a conservative, longer-range futures trader can get crushed.

One final point: If you know what time it is in trading, you don't have to be a slave to the quote machine, especially after the opening of whatever future you are looking at. You can check in at Fib Time intervals and be fairly confident you are keeping up with most of the action.

You can even (horrors!) junk that $600-a-month monster called the "quote service package." If you still want to chart intraday action, you can use 10-minute delayed quotes from a service like DTN Wall Street (1-800-485-4000), that hooks up to your computer and generates charts through an inexpensive software package. The total cost is only about $50 a month amortized over two years.

For those critical openings, you can use the quotes on CNBC's financial program, which would cost you nothing if you already have cable. You could back them up by a service like Infoline, provided by your discount broker. You simply dial an 800-number and get the latest quote. (If you want more information on Infoline, call First American Brokerage at 1-312-368-4700.)

According to a trader profile in *Futures* magazine, successful daytrader Gary Smith uses nothing for quotes except the ticker tape of CNBC, which gives him minute-by-minute quotes of the S&P 500. Says Gary, "I don't even know how to turn a computer on." Mindboggling!

But then again, not using a computer, isn't that what floor

traders do every day? Maybe Smith is beating the Mathematics of Investing not only because he is a remarkable trader but also because he doesn't have that big overhead other daytraders have.

"I am the only daytrader I know who can put on a position and take a nap," Smith says. Well, Mr. Smith, I've seen a lot of daytraders take a nap in my presence with positions on. They were called floor traders. But they did have their alarm clocks set for a certain time to wake up and go back into the pit to offset their positions.

If you can't take an occasional nap with a position on, no matter how short term that position, perhaps it's time for you to change trading styles. Knowing what time it is is the best way I know to achieve that peace of mind.

Chapter Nine

A Short Introduction to the Commercials

A few years ago I saw an ad by a firm that claimed to have found a way to provide econometric data to the futures market at a fraction of the $10,000- to $40,000-a-year per sector (grains, metals, currencies, etc.) typically charged by big names like Chase or Wharton for their big clients like banks, stock firms, grain processors, etc. (Econometrics is an attempt to program every known variable that might influence the price of something and predict future prices based on mathematical calculations. Or, as Webster defines it, the application of statistical methods to economic data and problems.)

Intrigued, I studied their track record over a few months' time and found out that, yes, their forecasts were very accurate over time. I agreed to join their firm to run their subscriber hotline. They would tell me which direction they believed a specific futures market was heading. Then I would apply trading techniques (like those described in this book) to give specific trade recommendations to their subscribers.

Our hotline gradually became so popular that in smaller markets (like cotton and platinum), our buy and sell recommendations were often the high or the low. Alas, all this came to an end when I found out how they were generating those great forecasts. They were making copies of the big-name econometric firms's reports housed in the Library of Congress in Washington, D.C. Plagiarizing the latest issues, they were able to keep abreast of the markets and make those remarkable forecasts.

There are software programs that claim to generate econometric forecasts, but the average PC is not going to be able to handle the thousands of variables and millions of calculations of an econometric program used by the biggies—even if you had time to program all those data entries. More importantly, no one has Chase or Wharton's political and economic connections to the centers of power—the Fed, Congress, etc. The results can be very impressive. For example, here are some of the highlights of a June 1987 executive summary of one of the big-name econometric firms:

1. A 1990 recession because of tightening by monetary authorities in response to escalating inflation and a phased-in tax increase in 1989–1990 to get the deficit under control.

2. Growth would be 0.6 percent in 1990 and then rebound to 4.7 percent in 1991 (the tax increase was not phased in but postponed until 1990. That's probably why these figures were a year off).

3. The dollar will rally from time to time, but will continue to go lower against the major currencies over the next 10 years (I think it is very likely that before 1998 the dollar index will go lower than its recent lows in September 1992).

Do you honestly think you are going to get is types of predictions from a software program costing a few hundred dollars?

Besides thorough knowledge of market fundamentals, commercials often have access to special intelligence well beyond the capability of the average trader, no matter how hard he studies the subject.

While I worked for the econometric firm described above, the Chernobyl nuclear reactor blew up. Fearing that half the wheat fields of Ukraine would be ruined with radioactivity, grains exploded, led by a limit up-move in wheat. The next day wheat was scheduled to go up another limit move, but my colleagues insisted I put out a sell recommendation on the hot-line. Wheat topped that day and promptly collapsed to below the price levels it was trading at before the Chernobyl incident occurred.

Later I found out why my colleagues were so confident. One of their friends from the CIA had called them up. "Don't worry about Chernobyl. We've seen the data from the spy satellites. The damage is very localized, only about 4 percent of Ukraine's wheat crop."

Not every commercial trader has a friend at the CIA, but most of them have very good sources of information totally unavailable to the public. In the case of Chernobyl, there was also data from a private, French commercial satellite called Spot. Spot's data may not have been as complete or processed as quickly as the CIA's multiple spy satellites, but rest assured the average commercial grain trader got the true facts of the situation well before the readers of *The Wall Street Journal*.

The largest privately held firm in the world is also the world's largest commercial grain dealer: Cargill. A privately held firm has an enormous disadvantage over publicly held businesses—it must raise all its capital internally or through bank borrowing (which carries interest costs far above dividends on common stock). But it also has one enormous advantage—it doesn't have to report a thing about its finances (or its trading practices) to the public.

Compared to floor traders, commercial traders are a secretive bunch that rarely tip their hand in public. But that stands to reason since even the biggest floor traders (such as Tom Baldwin) only compare in trading size to the smallest commercial traders. Commercials go to great lengths to disguise their trading lest any hint of their overall trading strategy create a buying or selling panic.

One favorite technique (among many) to disguise their trading intentions is the "give-up." Orders can be executed at one clearing firm and then given up at the end of the day to another. Cargill's broker may be selling 500,000 bushels of wheat while Merrill Lynch's brokers are buying 2 million. To all the world it appeared smart Cargill was selling grain while the dumb Merrill Lynch was buying for some dumb, technically oriented commodity fund. But, after trading hours, the 2 million bushels Merrill Lynch bought is given up (for a fee) to Cargill's account, making them net long 1.5 million bushels.

If commercials are willing to pay extra charges just to disguise their buying and selling, if they are paying millions in extra interest charges just to keep their trading activities from the public, why would they ever talk to you or me about their trading techniques?

Fortunately, there are ways—that don't cost $40,000 a year—that the public can follow these superb traders. I will outline some of them in the next four chapters. But before I do, I would like to give one word of caution: Just like floor traders have a better success record than the public, commercials on the whole trade better than the average floor trader (but perhaps not much better than veteran floor traders with many years of experience). However, individual commercial firms can be as dumb as any novice futures trader.

In the fall of 1993, reports started coming out that a major German industrial firm had lost hundreds of millions of dollars hedging in the crude oil market. Of course, when you read the fine print, this firm actually violated every principle of true hedging and was guilty of the worst kind of naked speculation. This multibillion dollar company certainly fit the government's definition of commercial trader. The average public trader would have been impressed if their broker had reported: "XYZ Gigantic firm is buying thousands of contracts of crude. Maybe we should go long, too."

Good trading, like good traders, should be felt but not seen. Once a megatrader becomes a household word like George Soros, you can be sure old George's public trading funds are headed for a fall (like their recent 25 percent dive). Similarly, if your broker says XYZ's buying (selling) is the talk of the street, it's a sure sign you want to be on the opposite side of the trade.

Occasionally, even smart commercial traders get fooled. From early June until mid-August of 1992, the commercials (as measured by the Commitment of Traders Report, more on this in the next chapter) began to go on a buying orgy. Ninety percent of the time this is a sign of a major bottom in commodity prices. But beginning in mid-August 1992, commercials gradually liquidated their long positions and became progressively more short. Then, in January 1993, a month before the recent bottom in the Commodity Research Bureau index CRB, they returned to their normal habit of buying a ton at bargain basement prices.

My contacts with commercial trading firms are slim. In any case, given their habitual secrecy, I doubt any man in America knows for sure exactly what made hundreds of commercial firms decide to abandon a profitable downtrend and go from being heavily net short to being net long. But there is one, huge coincidence that makes me fairly confident of the reason why.

In early June 1992, Perot's poll numbers began to slip and Clinton's numbers began to climb. By the start of August, Clinton had such a huge lead in the polls, it looked like the Democrats would sweep Congress. The Republicans would not be able to muster a filibuster in the Senate, and it would be "Carternomics" once again in America. (It was a Republican Senate filibuster that stopped Clinton's stimulus package).

Beginning in mid-August, Clinton's polls began to decline and, thanks to a successful convention, Bush was almost even with Clinton by September. By then, commercials could see that, whatever the fate of Bush, the Republicans were not going to lose big numbers in the Senate. They would be able to filibuster and stop many spending initiatives. The inflationary aspects of the Clinton presidency would be postponed.

All this goes to show that any one indicator can go wrong and you must have other things to back up your trading. But other than reading the media (which is the window to insider thinking), finding out what the commercials are doing (via the

Commitment of Traders report) is the indicator I respect the most. I am very, very reluctant to take positions contrary to what they are doing.

Chapter Ten

Reading Their Mail: The Commitment of Traders Report

The following report is by Jim Bianco CMT, chief analyst for Arbor Trading, a commercial bond trading firm. I've reprinted this report to give some idea of the incredibly accurate and timely information available to commercial traders and the importance of following the *Commitment of Traders* (*COT*) report.

Commentary for Friday October 1, 1993

Are Commodities the Trigger?

In last week's commentary (*Tulipmania*, September 23) we discussed the effect that the high rate of expansion in the adjusted monetary base is having on the bond market. We concluded: Eventually something will trigger a turnaround. Until then, a market that acts like a speculative bubble has considerable risk. Could commodity prices be that trigger?

First, some background. On May 28, the Federal Reserve moved to the much heralded asymmetric directive toward tightening. In English this meant that the Fed was worried about inflation and was prepared to do something about it. On August 17 (as it became known only last week), the Fed adopted a neutral directive. This means that the Fed no longer viewed inflation as an immediate problem.

In analyzing the message from financial markets leading up to these decisions, the story can be seen in the first chart (Figure 10-1). Gold and the CRB Index were rallying impressively going into the May 18 meeting. Similarly, in the weeks leading up to the August 17 meeting, gold and the CRB were declining. These were especially the case in the few days leading up to these meetings. Is the Fed drawing trendlines on commodity charts? [1]

We have argued for some time that commodity prices are the most important measure of inflation—especially the CRB. In supporting this claim, we have pointed out the high correlation between the CRB and bond yields (*This Time Is Not Different*—July 7). Therefore, if one gets a sense where the CRB is going, it provides a good insight into the direction of interest rates. Admittedly, bond yields and the CRB have recently diverged from their historical tendencies. This does not mean that the relationship is gone forever. The CRB is, and continues to be, an important measure of inflation despite the recent past.

---

[1] In 1966, Alan Greenspan wrote, ("Gold and Economic Freedom," *The Objectivist* magazine): "The law of supply and demand is not to be conned. As the supply of money increases relative to the supply of tangible assets in the economy, prices must eventually rise.... In the absence of the gold standard, there is no way to protect savings from confiscation through inflation." Yes, Virginia, our previous Fed governors were very aware of commodity trends. Unfortunately, Clinton's new Fed appointments are economic ignoramuses.

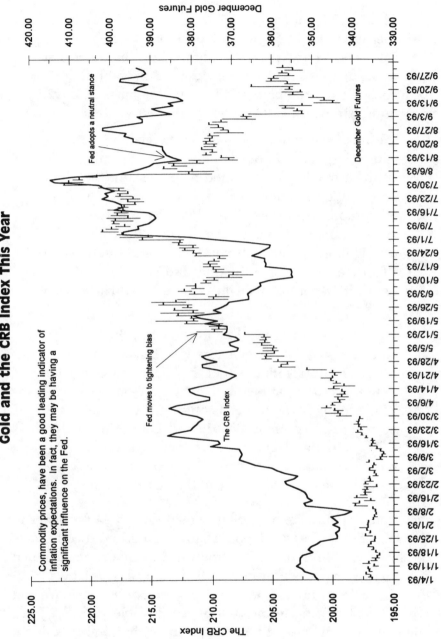

Figure 10-1
Gold and the CRB Index This Year

Commodity prices, have been a good leading indicator of inflation expectations. In fact, they may be having a significant influence on the Fed.

Fed adopts a neutral stance

Fed moves to tightening bias

The CRB Index

December Gold Futures

December Gold Futures

420.00
410.00
400.00
390.00
380.00
370.00
360.00
350.00
340.00
330.00

225.00
220.00
215.00
210.00
205.00
200.00
195.00

The CRB Index

1/4/93
1/11/93
1/18/93
1/25/93
2/1/93
2/8/93
2/16/93
2/23/93
3/2/93
3/9/93
3/16/93
3/23/93
3/30/93
4/6/93
4/14/93
4/21/93
4/28/93
5/5/93
5/12/93
5/19/93
5/26/93
6/3/93
6/10/93
6/17/93
6/24/93
7/1/93
7/9/93
7/16/93
7/23/93
7/30/93
8/6/93
8/13/93
8/20/93
8/27/93
9/3/93
9/13/93
9/20/93
9/27/93

Source: Glance Market Data Services

Are Commodities About to Head Higher?

Figure 10-2 shows the CRB/COT index. This index measures net long or short positions of commercial interests or hedgers in each of the 21 commodities that make up the CRB (a detailed description of this index's construction can be found in our September 21, 1992, and December 21, 1992, commentaries).

We track the activity of the commercial/hedgers because they have an outstanding record in calling the future direction of commodity prices. As the chart shows, the commercials/hedgers are again buying in all components of the CRB. This is especially true for gold. Also, their buying has now taken them above the dotted line shown on the chart. Had one bought when this index was above the line, and sold when it was below it, 78 percent of all these trades would have been profitable!

Since the August 1992 low in the CRB, the commercials/hedgers have reemerged as buyers at higher lows. The implication is that they are not waiting for new lows to be set before they step up and get long. This action, by definition, is bullish. If this analysis is correct, and commodities do indeed begin another upleg, inflation fears and asymmetric directives may return to haunt the bond market. In other words, commodities may yet again break the Fed trendlines.

You certainly are not going to read this type of analysis in *The Wall Street Journal*. Reporters for the normal media make $50,000 a year finding stories. Analysts like Bianco make much more trying to predict future trends. While *The Journal* was proclaiming a "New Era of Low Inflation" and *Barron's* was crowing about "Bonds Being in the Best of All Possible Worlds," Jim's clients had been warned for months about the coming collapse of bonds and explosion of prices (as measured by the CRB).

Figure 10–2
The CRB and the Hedgers

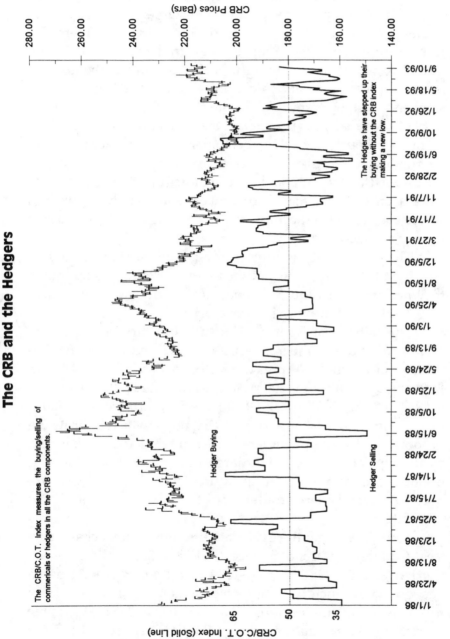

The CRB/C.O.T. Index measures the buying/selling of commericals or hedgers in all the CRB components.

CRB Prices (Bars)

CRB/C.O.T. Index (Solid Line)

Hedger Buying

Hedger Selling

The Hedgers have stepped up their buying without the CRB index making a new low.

The *COT* report is the best way to find out what commercials are doing. It's like reading their mail. Every two weeks the government tells you what positions the largest commercials are taking in the marketplace. The *COT* report divides traders into three groups. The first group is small traders who are not required to report their overnight positions daily to the government. Reportable positions can be as little as 50 contracts in smaller-volume futures to 850 contracts in the huge Eurodollar market. (Normally brokers report these positions to the government as a courtesy to their customers.) Those traders whose overnight contract size requires them to report their positions are divided further into large speculators (mostly futures funds since a majority of large floor brokers even up their holdings before each close) and commercials, who use the futures market mainly as a hedging vehicle.

The Commodity Futures Trading Commission (CFTC) issues the *COT* report, but since the report has become so popular, they no longer send out the report to individuals. So you have to get the report through intermediaries.

Through its data center, the Futures Industry Institute (FII's New York phone number is 1-202-223-1528) of the National Futures Association (NFA) puts out historical data of the *COT* from January 1986. The NFA (200 W. Madison, Suite 1600, Chicago, IL 60606-3447; 1-312-781-1300; 1-800-621-3570) through the FII also provides the CFTC's long-form *COT* reports, which indicate the proportion of total open interest in each regulated market held by the top four and top eight largest long and short reporting traders. In certain agricultural futures, this long-form *COT* report separates the large traders' positions by old crop and new crop futures.

You can also get the *COT* data through various chart services. Commodity Trend Service (P.O. Box 32309, Palm Beach Gardens, FL 33420; 1-800-331-1069; fax 1-407-622-7623) has a very good introductory pamphlet to the *COT* report titled, "How to Use Net Traders Positions." They also have the best graphic illustration of any chart service of the *COT* report and sell the data on the *COT* report like Pinnacle Data (below).

Pinnacle (460 Trailwood Ct., Webster, NY 14580; 1-800-724-4903; fax 1-716-872-1597) will send you the *COT* database of 42 futures back to January 1983 for $99. They also throw in a DataMaker software that can interpolate the semimonthly and the weekly values into daily values. (The CFTC used to collect the *COT* data twice a month, now it does so every two weeks).

For another $144 a year ($18 a month for diskette) you can get the *COT* data updated every two weeks by modem from Pinnacle. The CFTC releases two *COT* reports every other Friday at 3:30 P.M. covering the holdings at the close of the previous two Tuesdays. These two reports, along with updates to the *COT* database, are available for downloading by approximately 4:30 P.M. on those Fridays. A *COT* report can be downloaded in one minute at 4,800 baud; updates take approximately 10 seconds to download.

I have tried to minimize the need for computers in the techniques I discuss in this book. But if you are part of the computer generation, this data is a lot cheaper and far more valuable than any other futures software peddled on the market today.

In my introductory comments about the commercial trader, I stated that following the commercial trader through the *COT* is the indicator I respect the most next to following the media. But, like any single indicator, there are problems:

1. You are getting data that is three days behind the market, which can be an eternity in fast-moving markets. It's hard for the commercials to totally reverse their positions in three days, but this is still something for you to consider.

2. Now that the government is releasing this data every two weeks, this data has become very popular. *Barron's* and *The Wall Street Journal* have had major features on the *COT* report. Its popularity has become so great that the release of the *COT* has been credited with moving markets.

The April 1, 1994, *COT* report showed commercial traders had cut back their long positions in many commodities, notably precious metals, and increased their bearish short positions, as the May 2, 1994 *Wall Street Journal* article put it. "Its negative tone was widely cited as the cause of the rout (in commodities)," the article went on to say.

As a devoted follower of the print and electronic business media, I didn't see much evidence that the April 1, 1994, *COT* report was the cause for the fall in futures except in soybeans, which, in typical media trading fashion, were headed to a two-month low a few days later. But the point still stands. The more widely known and popular the indicator, the less value it is to the trader, who must find the charts no one sees.

3. The futures the *COT* report covers are not always the primary market for trading in that market.

Futures comprise less than 3 percent of the U.S. currency market, which in turn is not the primary market for world currency trading (London is). Any *COT* report about London-dominated futures has to be used with some caution.

During the last half of June 1994, gold commercials were reported in the *COT* to have begun to cover their shorts. They were at their most bullish reading since March 1993 by the August 12 report. Even a brilliant analyst like Bianco concluded: "Given their (the gold commercials) track record, we expect to see higher prices." While prices didn't collapse during the time commercials were becoming more bullish on gold, anyone piggybacking on their buying had to be somewhat disappointed. It may turn out that this was a great opportunity to buy gold but it also could be just another minor rally that fizzled at the $390–$410 level.

The silver commercials increased their short position short during June 1993, creating the largest short position for them in 10 years. The long position of the large traders in silver was the largest in ten years. Silver suffered over a 10 percent sell-off from late June to early August 1994.

Gold is mainly produced in South Africa and Russia and is mainly disposed of in Europe. U.S. gold commercials are relatively penny-ante compared to those in Europe. Even the best of them could be fooled concerning world market conditions. Silver is mainly produced in the western hemisphere (Mexico, Peru, Canada, the United States, Chile, etc.). The center of the silver trade is in New York. In other words, the commercials who have to report their futures trading to the government have their pulse directly on world demand because they are part of the primary market. They rarely, if ever, make mistakes.

When you use the *COT* Report, remember whether the dominant market is here or overseas. You should watch the commercials who are not part of the dominant market trade. They certainly know more than you and me. But they can get fooled, so trade accordingly.

4. Commercial traders are emotional human beings like every other trader. Unlike the public, they normally contain these emotions, but occasionally even they will yield to emotions and make dumb decisions.

In my introduction to the commercials, I discussed how they panicked and loaded up on everything when it seemed Clinton would bring in an era of free-spending Democrats. All they could see was a repeat of the Carter years when futures prices zoomed. But even during the Carter era, futures prices didn't go straight up immediately after Carter's inaugural. After 12 years of deflationary policies, even Clinton policies couldn't change things overnight. Any way you look at it, this was an overreaction.

But by far the worst example of emotional, dumb decisions by savvy commercial traders that I can think of was the secondary bond top in January 1994. The *COT* Report in bonds on January 4, 1994, showed commercial traders at the highest net long position since the August 1987 period, when bond prices were over 30 basis points lower. It was not that they weren't warned. As you can see from Bianco's report, many analysts were warning of collapse. Storm clouds were everywhere on the bond horizon, but the average commercial was blissfully loading up on bonds.

A very astute analyst, Paul Montgomery of Legg Mason, has made the observation that participants in a bull market become more concerned about their income statement than their balance sheet. This means that investors will take more risk because they fear a missed opportunity more than they fear potential loss of capital. Many commercial bond portfolio managers are in the same boat as their Wall Street counterparts. If the Street consensus said to buy and the portfolio manager does, and then stocks and bonds go down, the portfolio manager rarely gets in trouble. After all, he was only doing what everyone said was the smart thing to do.

But if the Street consensus is long and the manager does not follow it but stocks and bonds go up anyway, he is in deep trouble. The classic example is the stock managers who got out of the market in the spring of 1987 because stocks were getting far too frothy. Sitting in cash while the Dow soared from 2,300 to 2,700, they were crucified by their subscribers. They lost millions in assets as disgruntled investors rushed to invest with more stupid managers who only knew one way in the markets.

Even when the Dow plunged to 1630 in October 1987 and these managers were proven right, they rarely got back their previous investors. By that time these investors were too frightened to put money back into the stock market. If they didn't panic and sell out entirely, they left their money with the dumb managers because "Why should I make any moves now when things are so cheap?" Just like the special interests trample any legislator who really wants to represent his people by cutting spending, so the thundering emotions of Wall Street (and bond) investor insure they will always deserve a below average return.

You can't blame the failure of commercial bond traders on the fact they didn't trade the primary market. That's why I feel the media is the best indicator. The media were giddy, almost slaphappy in their reporting on the bond and stock market. Unlike even the best commercial traders, the media never fails to register a clear signal at major tops and bottoms.

Chapter Eleven

Spreads

There are two old floor trader definitions of a spread: a trade where you have twice the chance to lose, and the only position where two things have to go the right way for you to profit.

If you read all the interviews given by the traders quoted in *Market Wizards*,[1] spread trading seems to have caused more grief than anything else. In their early years, market wizards Bruce Kovnar, Brian Gelber, and Tony Saliba suffered massively from ill-conceived spreads.

Yet spreads are often the vehicle of choice for commercial traders (and many floor traders as well):

1. They provide relatively cheap insurance against some unexpected event that was beyond the capability of even the most astute commercial trader to anticipate.

You might have been able to anticipate the failed Russian coup attempt of August 1991 or the Chernobyl incident if you had a pipeline directly to the CIA. It's possible you could have anticipated, by observing the mysterious market movement just before these events, the sudden devaluation of the dollar by

---

1   Jack Schwager, *Market Wizards* (New York: Simon & Schuster, 1989)

Nixon in August 1971 or the Fed's shocking move to raise interest rates in a big way in November 1978. But if you hadn't and you were a commercial with large positions in the market, you could have suffered the loss of millions in a single stroke.

Now, as we've seen before, commercials can make awfully dumb decisions that have nothing to do with reality. But if you study all the evidence (I've provided you with just some if it with those charts in the *COT* section), you'll agree with me that these silly sessions are few and far between. No, the greatest enemy of the commercial is the unexpected event as outlined above.

Picture a commercial grain trader in August 1991 long a zillion bushels wheat. Unlike the floor trader or the funds, he didn't need to worry about position limits even if, strictly speaking, he was not hedging his future consumption needs. Prices were extraordinarily cheap, both after inflation and in nominal terms. The peak of the 18.6-year lunar node cycle (more on this in a later chapter) was due next year. The last time this cycle peaked, grain prices went berserk. Next year (1992) was an election year, and you know that politicians love to reward grain farmers in an election year—especially a presidential election year with all those farm state electoral votes. This commercial grain trader could anticipate the end of the harvest and the normal, strong seasonal uptrend in wheat prices. Yes, he could have anticipated everything but that a Russian coup attempt would send wheat prices down 20 cents in a day. Suddenly Russians were never going to eat wheat again and import our grain.

Of course, a commercial could have probably borrowed the money he needed for the margin call and ridden out the 10 weeks it took the wheat market to recover from this fiasco. Or he could have noted how much wheat had already rallied and purchased some insurance for a weekend surprise such as the Russian coup.

The margin on a wheat/corn spread never requires more margin than being net long wheat (usually it's less). He could have sold an equal amount of corn without putting out any more money for margin. Other than commissions (which is little more than floor fees for the average commercial), his only other cost was if a rally in corn cut slightly into his wheat profits. His only risk was the very, very slight chance that corn would go up faster than wheat in a time when wheat was almost all harvested but the corn harvest was yet to start.

Had he put on this insurance before the Russian coup, his losses after the coup would have been limited to the difference between the fall of wheat (20 cents) and the fall of corn (15 cents), or five cents total. It's likely he wouldn't have had to put in a dime more to hold this position. After the dust cleared and sanity returned to the markets, he could have quietly bought in his corn, went back to being net long wheat, and made a bundle over the next few months.

If the Fed chairman were to make some unprecedented advance announcement (as has happened) the whole yield curve could rise 10 basis points (a parallel shift) and the T-bond contract could lose 33 points without batting an eye. But if you had been short T-notes at the same time, the 21-point gain would have made up for a lot of that bond loss. And, like the wheat/corn situation above, putting on the same number of short T-note contracts as you have long bond contracts cost you nothing new in margin (usually it will cut it in half.

2. Spreads are often an easier way to take profits for the big commercials.

For professionals, taking losses are far easier than taking profits. Losses are mainly a mathematical problem—you can only lose so much based on the size of your account, so you take the loss. But taking a profit can be agony—who knows how far the market is going to go in your direction? After all, you've already decided that it is the right way it should go. Who are you to say it can't go any farther than X? Knowing when to take the profit is an art every professional trader is struggling to get exactly right.

Commercial traders have this problem, and one other besides: They are like elephants who have to watch where they step lest they crush the market. Putting on a spread often seems like the best solution to both problems.

Let's push our wheat commercial a few months ahead to December 1991. He's got big profits and wonders if it is time to sell. Just like the example above, the fundamentals of wheat are strong and the fundamentals of corn are weak. Rather than sell 10 million bushels of wheat outright, it's easier to sell five million wheat and five million corn at the same time.

In the first place, the commercial can test the market to see how it handles a large line of selling. If the market handles it well, he still has part of his wheat position left that should continue to outpace the short corn he has against it. If the market doesn't handle it well, he knows he was right to sell and goes ahead to sell the rest of his position, which takes down his short corn as well.

He won't make quite as much money being long five million wheat and short five million corn as he would by being net long 10 million bushels of wheat if wheat continues to rise. But if he found out he was right to be nervous about his wheat position, he got a jump on everyone else and didn't have to try to get out when the whole world was heading to the exit door.

One variation of this big-position testing process would be to simply sell corn and watch what happened to wheat. He doesn't tip his hand that he is nervous about his position and attract further selling. Nor does he overly compromise his potential profits as a wheat long. But he still gets to see the tone of the overall market.

3. Spreads are technically better than outright net positions.

The public, for the most part, does not look at spreads. The funds also consider them a minor vehicle. But any technique you would use on a bar chart—trend lines, retracements, gaps, etc.—works even better with spreads.

In fact, the herd buying and selling of funds creates tremendous spread opportunities. The funds and the public fixate on buying or selling one or two lead contracts. Thus the spreads distort from their true fundamentals. Being spread also enables floor traders and commercials to hold onto their core positions until the thundering herd gets done.

4. Changing spreads are one of the best warning indicators of a potential top or bottom.

There are three basic spread indicators at tops and bottoms.

a. *The weak sister approach.* This approach looks for a commodity in a sector (grains, meats, precious metals, etc.) that fails to go up, or goes up much less that the rest of the sector. When your analysis says sell the stronger futures, you sell the weak sister instead. If you are wrong, you won't lose much. But if you are right and the whole sector turns around, being short the weak sister might give you as many profits as being short some of the high flyers. This strategy works in reverse for a commodity that refuses to fall as fast as other futures in a weak sector.

b. *The lost leader approach.* Usually one commodity—or even one month in a commodity—leads the whole sector up or down. When, after a long period of leadership (several weeks at least) that leader suddenly fails to lead that sector on the up or downside, a trend change is likely for the whole sector.

This leader sometimes can be a leader in a sector for many years at a time. For a long while, gold shares have been leading the gold bullion market up and down. Utilities have been a good leading indicator for the direction on bonds. Soybean products (meal and oil) normally move ahead of soybeans (even if the soybean products movement warning is only a few hours ahead of the beans).

Smaller-volume futures that are dominated by commercial traders often initiate a move before the bigger members of the complex. "As oats go, so goes the grain market" is not true all the time. But it's true enough that it should be watched. I've also noticed palladium will often rally or fall before the other precious metals follow suit.

c. *Waiting for the end of the limits.* Often a sector will bottom or top (usually it's a top) when the last commodity of a sector comes off its limit and finally begins to trade after several days of limit moves (up or down).

Because commercials and floor traders are often spread between two commodities, they hesitate to take profits until both are freely trading and they can take off their spread as a spread. In addition, smart traders hesitate to move in or out of a position until they can read the spreads.

The Most Common Fallacy about Spreads

The most common fallacy about spreads is that they are not net positions. No, I'm not being facetious. What I mean by this is that it is important to calculate spreads in percentage terms and not as absolute numbers.

Look at any spread chart that records the history of spreads for several decades. If July beans are 25 cents over November beans (the July contract is 25 cents higher), and it moves to 50 cents over November, recorded in the spread chart history is this 25-cent move.

It matters not if this occurred because November beans were 5.00 and stayed 5.00 while July went from 5.25 to 5.50, or if November beans were 7.00 and went to 10.00 while July went from 7.25 to 10.50. Yet we all know intuitively that these are different situations and shouldn't be viewed the same way.

In the first 25-cent spread move, July went from 5 percent over November to 10 percent. In the second identical move, July was 3.57 percent over November and went to 5 percent over. They are not the same.

In the 1950s through the early 1970s, corn traded mainly in a trading range from 1.60 a bushel to a little above a 1.00 a bushel. If we look at a historical corn basis chart (the difference between the closest future and a primary cash market), is a five-cent basis the same as a five-cent basis now? But that's what every basis chart I've seen implies.

One thing is apparent to me. If anyone is going to do historical spread comparisons, he should use percentage terms rather nominal moves—even though the spread trader is paid off in nominal terms. Otherwise, how does he know if a spread move is normal or not?

You don't suffer from this type of price illusion when you compare the price history of a single future. A 10.00 to 11.00 move in the nominal charts is the same in 1974 or 1994 (although what it means after inflation and currency factors are taken into account are another matter altogether).

A 5.00 to 6.00 move is 20 percent, while the same one-dollar move from 10.00 to 11.00 is only 10 percent, but this distortion is readily adjusted for on the nominal chart through trend lines that rise and fall at a constant percentage and other similar technical indicators.

But when it comes to spreads, if you attempt to do research on them in the exchanges, through commercial vendors of historical data, or in books, you see spreads treated the same way as single futures—the spread price difference is the spread price difference is the spread price difference. Any conversion of them to a ratio that is measured by percentages, instead of differences in the prices, has to be done by you.

What if I told you that the ratio of the Dow to the CRB is the highest in history, that this ratio is nearly double that of the mid-1960s? That's a significant statistic you can understand. You can even chart this ratio and use it for some of your long-term decision making.

But what if I said the Dow-to-CRB spread is +3670? That may be technically correct, but can you use it for comparisons? Does this figure help you in long-term decision making? Yet traders do this all the time in researching data on spreads!

The investment world is full of spreads, only they are called "ratios" when they are not directly traded on some exchange (i.e., the option premium ratio between the premium on calls versus the premium on puts), or the standard put/call ratio and all the variations thereof. These may be called sentiment indicators, but they are really spread relationships, ratios that historically have high and low readings. I could go on and on giving examples of financial spreads.

Now, I believe the media is the best trading indicator there is, but in accordance with the Psychological Rule of 10/20 Percent, I would never base any more than 20 percent of my trading decisions on what the media is saying to do in the market. Otherwise I am vulnerable to being overly committed to one course of action, refusing to change my opinion and read the changes in the market, which might even be (ever so subtlety) being reflected by the media as well. Like Longstreet's trader, I've entered the Hall of Mirrors: everything I see only encourages me to believe I am a trading genius that has found the secret of the trading universe.

In regard to the Psychological Rule of 10/20 Percent, a spread is a spread is a spread. If you are using ratios like the put/call, you are still basing your trading decision on a spread. You are still relying on historical relationships between two things. So be on your guard that you aren't overly committed in your analysis to spreads. It's an easy thing to do, especially for professionals that are constantly looking for another way to look at data.

As I look over the last few pages, I can see I've spent a lot time warning about the misuse of spreads. I may have inadvertently given too negative an impression on the use of spreads in your trading and your analysis.

The fact is, I love to read about and look at spreads. It's the second most powerful tool in determining what commercial traders might be doing. Compared to all the "Trading Secrets of the Universe" books out there, little has been written about spreads. I advise you to read all the books you can find about spreads and spend time looking at their charts. By all means, you should be on the lookout for ratios in the market that few know about. Just keep my warning in mind when you do so.

Chapter Twelve

Real-World Investing— It's Not "All in the Charts"

According to *Commodity Futures Trading: A Biographical Guide*, R.N. Elliott was a mystic who believed mathematical relationships in an Egyptian pyramid predicted future events and corroborated his own wave theory.[1] W.D. Gann's books are full of references to numerology and what can only be called a weird mixture of Bible and astrology.

These two pillars of technical analysis are by no means unique. Pick up financial publications, especially those specializing in futures, and you will see advertisements for everything from financial astrology to mind-numbing esoteria like twin-vibration vertical-bar backtracking system that needs a computer genius to run and Ph.D. to understand. Whether you call it the Sacred Six or Chart Mysticism, the belief that price-only analysis is the key to trading success has captured the overwhelming majority of futures traders.

---

1   James B. Way, *Commodity Futures Trading: A Biographical Guide* (New York: R. R. Banker, 1976).

My first encounter with this religion was in 1977. It was my second job as a broker. I worked for a clearing firm of the Chicago Mercantile Exchange. A computerized charting system had just been installed in the bowels of the building that housed the Exchange. From this specially air-conditioned room (whenever the air conditioning broke down, the computer was shut off), terminals all over the building received those magical charts. Think of it! It was less than 20 years ago, but the average broker was still depending on those grimy charts that came out once a week. As for intraday charts, floor traders constructed them by hand from little notes they scribbled on their trading cards. It was a big deal to get spread charts from the only service that handled them. Today, virtually every futures trader has all this and more at the stroke of a key. But I remember how everyone in the office spent hours, totally mesmerized, pouring over the charts and indicators that came effortlessly to the screen. Who could possibly lose in this brave new world of instant technical analysis?

Sadly, all this computerized technical firepower has not changed the loss ratio of the average futures trader. Ninety percent of them are still losing, a percentage mainly due to the factors discussed in the second chapter of this book.

But even technicians that have mastered the psychological and mathematical pitfalls of trading still have another obstacle in their path. The very price data they depend on is flawed in at least three basic ways:

1. The big money—the major players that move the market—may be looking at something entirely different than futures prices.

In currency it's cross rates, in interest rates it's yields, and in the stock market, decisions are being made based on the cash prices of individual stocks and stock indexes. The carrying charge factor built into the futures price of both stock indexes and bond futures does cause distortion.

Jim Bianco, Arbor Trading's brilliant analyst, uses the Lehman Long-Treasury Index in his long-term analysis. This index is a market-weighted index of all Treasury issues between 10 and 30 years and is not distorted by the positive carrying charge of futures nor the on-the-run bonds like a yield chart. No wonder futures bond trading can be so frustrating technically!

2. The price action of stocks is different than that of futures; a bear market reacts differently than a bull market.

I've discussed this in detail in several previous chapters, but it's worth noting again that most of the classic works of technical analysis were designed for stock trading, not for futures.

3. The great technical gurus of the past (Gann, Elliott, Andrews, Edwards and McGee, etc.) operated in a stable environment of level prices and fixed currencies.

According to a study by Warren and Pearson, wholesale prices in 1910-1914 were virtually identical to those in 1793, one year before the start of U.S. gold coinage. This remarkable price stability was marred only by the War of 1812 and the Civil War. To pay for those wars, the Treasury issued fiat currency in the form of Treasury notes and greenbacks. Prices doubled, but soon returned to normal when gold and silver coins were minted again after these wars. All this has changed, due to the following factors:

1. Senators are no longer elected by state legislatures, but directly by the people. Gradually, the power of state governments was eroded to the point that today, they are becoming mere rubber stamps of the federal government. (If you don't believe me, just ask your state legislator how much of your state's budget is driven by Federal matching funds or mandates.) The ninth and tenth amendments of the Constitution became dead letters. States can't issue money, but the federal government can. Through the Federal Reserve System, this debt can be "monetized" and inflated away. Thus the federal government has a great incentive to expand, spend money, and go into debt—the cost of which is passed on

to the American people as a tax called inflation.

2. The sixteenth amendment allowing a federal income tax gave the Feds a great tool to expand their tax base, which was previously based on the very limited revenues of customs. A big government with a big tax base can maintain a big debt—which gives the government every incentive to inflate that big debt away.

3. The founding of the Federal Reserve—a private bank—let the politicians blame recessions, depressions, and inflation on someone else. No longer would monetary transactions be under public scrutiny at the U.S. Treasury.

In 1913, the Fed was required to have a 40 percent gold backing on the Federal Reserve notes it issued, 35 percent for system liabilities. In 1945, this was reduced to 25 percent as the Bretton Woods Agreement officially abolished the old gold standard. In 1965, the Fed was no longer required to have gold backing on system liabilities. By 1968, all gold-backing requirements were removed from Federal Reserve notes, and silver certificates were no longer valid. In August 1971, the last link with gold was severed when Nixon suspended balance of payments in gold to overseas' governments and let the dollar float.

After each of these actions, inflation ratcheted upward. Today, we congratulate ourselves that inflation is only 3 percent—just like we are pleased the federal deficit will only be $160 billion or the crime bill was cut from $33 billion to $30 billion, or the dollar rallied a few percentage points after losing half its value in a decade. There is really no sign that inflation, government spending, or monetary chaos is going to stop.

But most chartists would rather die than admit their sacred charts need to take account of currency- and inflation-adjusting fundamentals. It's easier to talk about an "unexpected Elliott-Wave extension or Gann number I forgot." The last 50 years have seen unprecedented inflation and currency fluctuations, yet the same old charting practices of the 1930s and 1940s are still taught as gospel. If McGee and Edwards were still writing, they'd use inflation- and currency-adjusted charts!

I could give hundreds of examples of where inflation- and currency-adjusted charts were more accurate in determining future price trends than nominal charts. I can only hope the few examples I give in this book will somehow jolt you out of the nominal chart orthodoxy and into looking at inflation- and currency-adjusted charts.

One Example of Inflation-Adjusted Charting

Figure 12-1 is the "Constant Dollar Dow" put out by Media General Financial Services of Richmond Virginia. On the top half you see the nominal price of the Dow. On the bottom is the inflation-adjusted, Constant Dollar Dow.

The Constant Dollar Dow has been far more accurate in calling Dow tops than standard technical analysis. Few technicians were calling for a top in August 1987, but the 1.382 gap objective in the Constant Dollar Dow chart was almost exactly the August 1987 top (March 1986 gap of 143.02 minus the August 1982 low of 78.01 = 65.01; 65.01 × 1.382 + 143.02 = 232.86). The 1987 move also filled a gap made in February 1973 at 228.60.

In January 1994 the Constant Dollar Dow went over 260, filling a gap at 252.71 and reaching the secondary, reaction high of 261.32 of May 1969. A classic three-wave, C-wave Elliott correction was being completed.

But most technicians at the time were saying 4,000 in the nominal Dow would be easily breached. They urged you to buy any small correction. I can still hear the voice of our local TV Elliottician: "I just looooove these corrections."

After missing the top in January, most technicians in April were expecting even lower stock prices. But the next Constant Dollar Dow support level was at the 235-240 level. (We reached a Constant Dollar Dow low of 238.91 on April 4, 1994.) In the real world of constant dollars, it was time to buy.

I doubt if these technicians would have been so off if they had been looking at real-world constant dollar charts. Nor is it likely they'd be so excited at the recent August 1994 technical breakout of the stock market if they saw the trend line off the 1966 high and the January 1994 high in the Constant Dollar Dow.

Figure 12–1
The Constant Dollar Dow

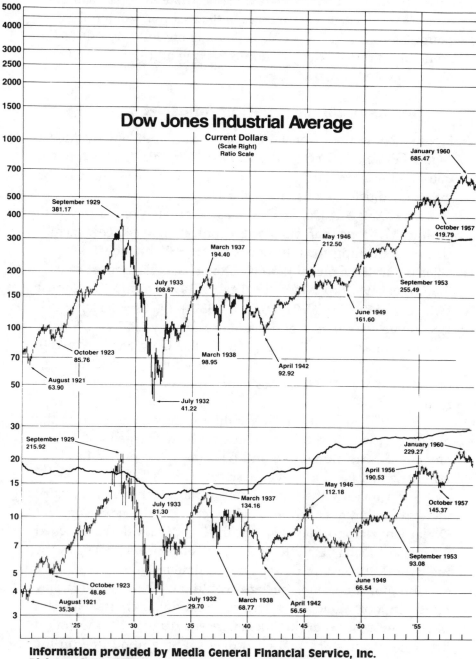

Dow Jones Industrial Average

Current Dollars
(Scale Right)
Ratio Scale

January 1960
685.47

September 1929
381.17

October 1957
419.79

March 1937
194.40

May 1946
212.50

July 1933
108.67

September 1953
255.49

June 1949
161.60

October 1923
85.76

March 1938
98.95

April 1942
92.92

August 1921
63.90

July 1932
41.22

September 1929
215.92

January 1960
229.27

April 1956
190.53

May 1946
112.18

March 1937
134.16

July 1933
81.30

October 1957
145.37

October 1923
48.86

September 1953
93.08

August 1921
35.38

July 1932
29.70

March 1938
68.77

April 1942
56.56

June 1949
66.54

**Information provided by Media General Financial Service, Inc.
Richmond, Inc. 23293**

Figure 12–1
The Constant Dollar Dow (continued)

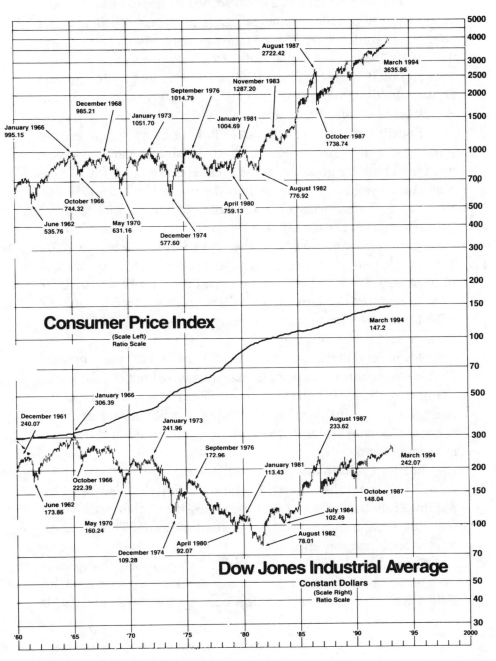

It's time to sell, not buy.

If you look at the 1932–1966 record of the Constant Dollar Dow, you see it matches the teachings of the Elliotticians better than the nominal chart. There is the impressively dynamic Wave 1 of 1932–1937. Next is the Wave 2 (which retraces so much of Wave 1) of 1937–1942. Third Waves are wonders to behold and so was the dynamic move from 1942 to 1960 (which in turn has the classic five-way structure).

Fourth Waves more often than not are complex waves. The gyrations in the early 1960s of the Constant Dollar Dow were gut-wrenching for investors at the time. The average Fifth Wave is almost always less impressive than the third. The 1962–1966 bull market was a solid advance, but nothing like the glorious 1950s.[2]

If you look at the Constant Dollar Dow from 1982–1994, the classic pattern continues, a near-perfect miniature of the 1932–1966 stock pattern. After the Crash of 1987, while prominent Elliotticians like Bob Prechter were calling for a repeat of 1929, I wrote a report to clients that was later summarized in the June 1988 issue of *Futures* magazine. In it I stated my belief that the Dow would make new highs.

My interpretation of the Elliott Wave using the Constant Dollar Dow chart was one of the reasons why I felt the Dow was going to make new highs after the 1987 crash. It's also one of the reasons why I think the Dow has made a multiyear top and will continue to slide (at least after inflation is factored out) over the next few years.

Earlier I said that if the great masters were alive, they'd be using constant dollar charts. Certainly Elliott was aware of inflation. "Elliott contended that the necessity of channeling on a semi-log scale indicated the presence of inflation. This assumption is demonstrably incorrect."[3]

Typical of the "pick-and-choose-what-you-like" disciples of the great technical masters, Frost and Prechter went on to claim Elliott was wrong about inflation because the 1920s and 1930s

---

2   Frost, Prechter, *The Elliott Wave Principle* (Gainesville, GA: New Classics Library, 1977).
3   *Ibid.*

were a time of deflation. But perhaps the great master was thinking about the big price rise since 1896 even as he drew his charts in the 1920s and 1930s. He intuitively picked up that the twentieth century would be an inflation century, and that the 1920s and 1930s were only an aberration.

Frost and Prechter later went on to reprint an inflation-adjusted chart in the *Elliott Wave Principle* (Figure 12-2), so they couldn't plead ignorance of how inflation adjusting is necessary on long-term charts. Why did they ignore inflation adjusting in the rest of their book? Why, despite the humiliation of their post-1987-crash predictions, do most of the prominent Elliotticians continue to avoid the subject today?

Inflation adjusting does adds an element of (temporary) confusion. Investors have to be taught how to look at inflation-adjusted charts to make long-range decisions and still make their money in nominally denominated markets.

But in my opinion, the main stumbling block is Chart Mysticism. How can I be the big technical guru if I have to admit some obvious fundamental is affecting my charts? If something as mundane as inflation has to be watched, maybe, just maybe, it really isn't true that all we need to know is in the charts! Maybe I need to get another guru who knows something else.

I believe investors should look at inflation-adjusted charts in every future they are trading. You can hardly do effective long-term analysis without them. But because inflation figures come out once a month, inflation-adjusted charts have to be monthly. A month is an eternity for most traders, so I won't spend any more time discussing inflation-adjusting charts other than to give you a simple method to construct them.

Each month the Bureau of Labor Statistics comes out with the Consumer Price Index average for all urban consumers (CPI-U). This number is widely reported in the business press. The Bureau also has regional offices in Boston, New York, Philadelphia, Atlanta, Chicago, Dallas, Kansas City, and San Fransisco where you can get monthly CPI updates through the main number or on a CPI hotline. The CPI numbers since January 1913 until the day of this writing are given in Figure 12-3 as a courtesy to the reader.

Figure 12-2

The Grand Supercycle (year-end closing prices, semilog scale)

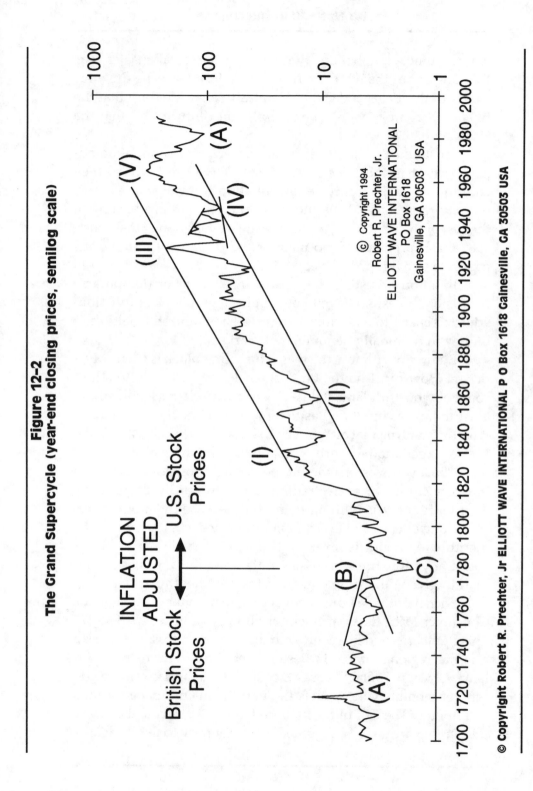

Figure 12-3
CPI (1982-1984 = 100)

Year	Jan.	Feb.	Mar.	Apr.	May	June	July	Aug.	Sept.	Oct.	Nov.	Dec.
1913	9.8	9.8	9.8	9.8	9.7	9.8	9.9	9.9	10.0	10.0	10.1	10.0
1914	10.8	9.9	9.9	9.8	9.9	9.9	10.0	10.2	10.2	10.1	10.2	10.1
1915	10.1	10.0	9.9	10.0	10.1	10.1	10.1	10.1	10.1	10.2	10.3	10.3
1916	10.4	10.4	10.5	10.6	10.7	10.8	10.8	10.9	11.1	11.3	11.5	11.6
1917	11.7	12.0	12.8	12.6	12.8	13.0	12.8	13.0	13.3	13.5	13.5	13.7
1918	14.0	14.1	14.0	14.2	14.5	14.7	15.1	15.4	15.7	16.0	16.3	16.5
1919	16.5	16.2	16.4	16.7	16.9	16.9	17.8	17.7	17.8	18.1	18.5	18.9
1920	19.3	19.5	19.7	20.3	20.6	20.9	20.8	20.3	20.0	19.9	19.8	19.4
1921	19.0	18.4	18.3	18.1	17.7	17.6	17.7	17.7	17.5	17.5	17.4	17.3
1922	16.9	16.9	16.7	16.7	16.7	16.7	16.8	16.6	16.6	16.7	16.8	16.9
1923	16.8	16.8	16.8	16.9	16.9	17.0	17.1	17.0	17.1	17.2	17.2	17.3
1924	17.3	17.2	17.1	17.0	17.0	17.0	17.1	17.0	17.1	17.2	17.2	17.3
1925	17.3	17.2	17.3	17.2	17.3	17.5	17.7	17.7	17.7	17.7	18.0	17.9
1926	17.9	17.9	17.8	17.9	17.8	17.7	17.5	17.4	17.5	17.6	17.7	17.7
1927	17.5	17.4	17.3	17.3	17.4	17.6	17.3	17.2	17.3	17.4	17.3	17.3
1928	17.3	17.1	17.1	17.1	17.2	17.1	17.1	17.1	17.3	17.2	17.2	17.1
1929	17.1	17.1	17.0	16.9	17.0	17.1	17.3	17.3	17.3	17.3	17.3	17.2
1930	17.1	17.0	16.9	17.0	16.9	16.8	16.6	16.5	16.6	16.5	16.4	16.1
1931	15.9	15.7	15.6	15.5	15.3	15.1	15.1	15.1	15.0	14.9	14.7	14.6
1932	14.3	14.1	14.0	13.9	13.7	13.6	13.6	13.5	13.4	13.3	13.2	13.1
1933	12.9	12.7	12.6	12.6	12.6	12.7	13.1	13.2	13.2	13.2	13.2	13.2
1934	13.2	13.3	13.3	13.3	13.3	13.4	13.4	13.4	13.6	13.5	13.5	13.4
1935	13.6	13.7	13.7	13.8	13.8	13.7	13.7	13.7	13.7	13.7	13.8	13.8
1936	13.8	13.8	13.7	13.7	13.7	13.8	13.9	14.0	14.0	14.0	14.0	14.0
1937	14.1	14.1	14.2	14.3	14.4	14.4	14.5	14.5	14.6	14.6	14.5	14.4
1938	14.2	14.1	14.1	14.2	14.1	14.1	14.1	14.1	14.1	14.0	14.0	14.0
1939	14.0	13.9	13.9	13.8	13.8	13.8	13.8	13.8	14.1	14.0	14.0	14.0
1940	13.9	14.0	14.0	14.0	14.0	14.1	14.0	14.0	14.0	14.0	14.0	14.1
1941	14.1	14.1	14.2	14.3	14.4	14.7	14.7	14.9	15.1	15.3	15.4	15.5
1942	15.7	15.8	16.0	16.1	16.3	16.3	16.4	16.5	16.5	16.7	16.8	16.9

Figure 12-3
CPI (1982-1984 = 100) (continued)

Year	Jan.	Feb.	Mar.	Apr.	May	June	July	Aug.	Sept.	Oct.	Nov.	Dec.
1943	16.9	16.9	17.2	17.4	17.5	17.5	17.4	17.3	17.4	17.4	17.4	17.4
1944	17.4	17.4	17.4	17.5	17.5	17.6	17.7	17.7	17.7	17.7	17.7	17.8
1945	17.8	17.8	17.8	17.8	17.9	18.1	18.1	18.1	18.1	18.1	18.1	18.2
1946	18.2	18.1	18.3	18.4	18.5	18.7	19.8	20.2	20.4	20.8	21.3	21.5
1947	21.5	21.5	21.9	21.9	21.9	22.0	22.2	22.5	23.0	23.0	23.1	23.4
1948	23.7	23.5	23.4	23.8	23.9	24.1	24.4	24.5	24.5	24.4	24.2	24.1
1949	24.0	23.8	23.8	23.9	23.8	23.9	23.7	23.8	23.9	23.7	23.8	23.6
1950	23.5	23.5	23.6	23.6	23.7	23.8	24.1	24.3	24.4	24.6	24.7	25.0
1951	25.4	25.7	25.8	25.8	25.9	25.9	25.9	25.9	26.1	26.2	26.4	26.5
1952	26.5	26.5	26.3	26.4	26.4	26.5	26.7	26.7	26.7	26.7	26.7	26.7
1953	26.6	26.5	26.6	26.6	26.7	26.8	26.8	26.9	26.9	27.0	26.9	26.9
1954	26.9	26.9	26.9	26.8	26.9	26.9	26.9	26.9	26.8	26.8	26.8	26.7
1955	26.7	26.7	26.7	26.7	26.7	26.7	26.8	26.8	26.9	26.9	26.9	26.8
1956	26.8	26.8	26.8	26.9	27.0	27.2	27.4	27.3	27.4	27.5	27.5	27.6
1957	27.6	27.7	27.8	27.9	28.0	28.1	28.3	28.3	28.3	28.3	28.4	28.4
1958	28.6	28.6	28.8	28.9	28.9	28.9	29.0	28.9	28.9	28.9	29.0	28.9
1959	29.0	28.9	28.9	29.0	29.0	29.1	29.2	29.2	29.3	29.4	29.4	29.4
1960	29.3	26.4	29.4	29.5	29.5	29.6	29.6	29.6	29.6	29.8	29.8	29.8
1961	29.8	29.8	29.8	29.8	29.8	29.8	30.0	29.9	30.0	30..0	30..0	30.0
1962	30.0	30.1	30.1	30.2	30.2	30.2	30.3	30.3	30.3	30.4	30.4	30.4
1963	30.4	30.4	30.5	30.5	30.5	30.6	30.7	30.7	30.7	30.8	30.8	30.9
1964	30.9	30.9	20.9	20.9	30.9	21.0	31.1	31.0	31.1	31.1	31.2	31.2
1965	31.2	31.2	31.3	31.4	31.4	31.6	31.6	31.6	31.6	31.7	31.7	31.8
1966	31.8	32.0	32.1	32.3	32.3	32.4	32.5	32.7	32.7	32.9	32.9	32.9
1967	32.9	32.9	33.0	33.1	33.2	33.3	33.4	33.5	33.6	33.7	33.8	33.9
1968	34.1	34.2	34.3	34.4	34.5	34.7	34.9	35.0	35.1	35.3	35.4	35.5
1969	35.6	35.8	36.1	36.3	36.4	36.6	36.8	37.0	37.1	37.3	37.5	37.7
1970	37.8	38.0	38.2	38.5	38.6	38.8	39.0	39.0	39.2	39.4	39.6	39.8
1971	39.8	39.9	40.0	40.1	40.3	40.6	40.7	40.8	40.8	40.9	40.9	41.1
1972	41.1	41.3	41.4	41.5	41.6	41.7	41.9	42.0	42.1	42.3	42.4	42.5

Figure 12-3
CPI (1982-1984 = 100) (continued)

Year	Jan.	Feb.	Mar.	Apr.	May	June	July	Aug.	Sept.	Oct.	Nov.	Dec.
1973	42.6	42.9	43.3	43.6	43.9	44.2	44.3	45.1	45.2	45.6	45.9	46.2
1974	46.6	47.2	47.8	48.0	48.6	49.0	49.4	50.0	50.6	51.1	51.5	51.9
1975	52.1	52.5	52.7	52.9	53.2	53.6	54.2	54.3	54.6	54.9	55.3	55.5
1976	55.6	55.8	55.9	56.1	56.5	56.8	57.1	57.4	57.6	57.9	58.0	58.2
1977	58.5	59.1	59.5	60.0	60.3	60.7	61.0	61.2	61.4	61.6	61.9	62.1
1978	62.5	62.9	63.4	63.9	64.5	65.2	65.7	66.0	66.5	67.1	67.4	67.7
1979	68.3	69.1	69.8	70.6	71.5	72.3	73.1	73.8	74.6	75.2	75.9	76.7
1980	77.8	78.9	80.1	81.0	81.8	82.7	82.7	83.3	84.0	84.8	85.5	86.3
1981	87.0	87.9	88.5	89.1	89.8	90.6	91.6	92.3	93.2	93.4	93.7	94.0
1982	94.3	94.6	94.5	94.9	95.8	97.0	97.5	97.7	97.9	98.2	98.0	97.6
1983	97.8	97.9	97.9	98.6	99.2	99.5	99.9	100.2	100.7	101.0	101.2	101.3
1984	101.9	102.4	102.6	103.1	103.4	103.7	104.1	104.5	105.0	105.3	105.3	105.3
1985	105.5	106.0	106.4	106.9	107.3	107.6	107.8	108.0	108.3	108.7	109.0	109.3
1986	109.6	109.3	108.8	108.6	108.9	109.5	109.5	109.7	110.2	110.3	110.4	110.5
1987	111.2	111.6	112.1	112.7	113.1	113.5	113.8	114.4	115.0	115.3	115.4	115.4
1988	115.7	116.0	116.5	117.1	117.5	118.0	118.5	119.0	119.8	120.2	120.3	120.5
1989	121.1	121.6	122.3	123.1	123.8	124.1	124.4	124.6	125.0	125.6	125.9	126.1
1990	127.4	128.0	128.7	128.9	129.2	129.9	130.4	131.6	132.7	133.5	133.8	133.8
1991	134.6	134.8	135.0	135.2	135.6	136.0	136.2	136.6	137.2	137.4	137.8	137.9
1992	138.1	138.6	139.3	139.5	139.7	140.2	140.5	140.9	141.3	141.8	142.0	141.9
1993	142.6	143.1	143.6	144.0	144.2	144.4	144.4	144.8	145.1	145.7	145.8	145.8
1994	146.2	146.7	147.2	147.4	147.5	148.0	148.4	149.0				

To calculate an inflation-adjusted chart, simply divide the CPI monthly figure by each of the open, high, low, and close of the same month's nominal numbers of the future you are working with. To avoid fractional outcomes, you may want to shift the decimals on the CPI numbers one or two spaces to the left. Here's how it would work using a hypothetical (but very close to reality) gold example:

Gold is 35.00 an ounce in August 1970. The CPI in August

1970 is 39, which for purposes of an easier notation we will call .39. We then divide 35 by .39 to create an inflation-adjusted gold price of 89.74 for August 1970 gold.

The February 1985 gold price is 290. Since the CPI in February 1985 was 106, we divide 290 by 1.06 (using the same two-decimal-point shift) to get an inflation-adjusted or constant dollar gold price of 273.58.

As you can see, while the nominal price of gold ballooned over eight times from August 1970 to February 1985, the real price of gold actually increased less than three-and-a-half times. Do you still pay 25 cents a gallon for gas? A nickel for a daily newspaper? Then why are you still using charts and market-timing methods from that era?

Currency-Adjusted Charting

Unlike inflation, currency fluctuations can be easily tracked on a daily, even minute-by-minute, basis. In the impatient world of the futures trader, currency-adjusted charts can give you immediate feedback on the real-world price of a future. In a way, currency fluctuations have replaced inflation as the prime variable in real-world charting. Since October 1980, the dollar as measured by the U.S. dollar index has fluctuated over 260 percent, while inflation has been up a mere 75 percent. This trend has been accelerating in recent years.

For these two reasons, I am going to spend the rest of this chapter and most of my examples of real-world investing on currency-adjusted charts. Despite all the talk of a Unified European Currency and Trade Block Currency Mechanisms, world currencies continue to bob up and down as fast as they have during the last 25 years.

Our first problem in currency adjusting is which currency to use. I brushed over a similar problem in inflation adjusting (some use wholesale prices or even the price of gold) because the consensus is pretty much centered on the Consumer Price Index as the adjustment mechanism of choice. But adjusting by currency factors is a lot trickier.

One prominent Certified Market Technician (CMT) I know uses Special Drawing Rights (SDR). The SDR is an index developed by the International Monetary Fund based on a weighted basket of the currencies of the five largest exporting countries. The recent weighting of this basket was the U.S. dollar 42 percent, German mark 19 percent, Japanese yen 15 percent, French franc 12 percent, British pound 12 percent.

Conversion of any asset's price into its SDR value is accomplished by dividing the asset price by the SDR rate for the currency in which the price is quoted. The U.S. dollar conversion rate is listed in each issue of the *Financial Times* of London, *Barron's*, and *The Wall Street Journal* under Foreign Exchange Rates or Exchange Rates.

The easiest available source of daily quotes for the SDR is at the bottom (along with that other currency hybrid, the European Currency Unit or ECU) of the Exchange Rate box somewhere in section C of *The Wall Street Journal*. By taking that number (say 1.38612) and dividing it by a future's price (350 gold), you get an SDR price of 252.50 for gold.

While the SDR can be followed quite easily in *The Wall Street Journal*, it's still overweighted to the dollar. The purpose of currency adjusting is to get an idea of how foreigners view our assets—are they cheap or expensive? Even SDR's big five currencies barely scratch the surface of world trade. And there are other technical flaws like the absurd notion that the French economy is only a little less than the Japanese economy.

Some argue that a yen/mark index could be constructed to currency adjust our dollar-denominated futures markets. The Japanese yen and the German mark are the lead currencies of Asia and Europe, respectively. Combined, the economies of Japan and Germany are nearly that of the United States. Their currencies are starting to take the place of the dollar as the lead reserve currencies in their areas. Indeed, some would argue the dollar standard set up in Bretton Woods in 1944 has already been replaced by a mark/yen standard, thanks to the distrust of U.S. inflationary policies.

As big as the Japanese and German economies are, as much as they export and invest in the United States, they still only account for a fraction (a big fraction, I grant you) of the investment and foreign trade in this country and of dollar assets overseas. In addition, a simple average of the two currencies (for example, by adding the two futures or Forex quotes) would not reflect trading and investment realities (i.e., the Japanese are much more influential than the German in our economy).

That's why I feel the U.S. dollar index has to be the currency-adjusting mechanism. It represents 15 foreign currencies, not just the five of the SDR. You can get the U.S. dollar index on a minute-by-minute basis like the Japanese yen and German mark Forex/Future quotes, but it's also trade-weighted. There are other trade-weighted indexes, but they are not readily available like the U.S. dollar index.

Constructing currency-adjusted charts with the U.S. dollar index is similar to inflation adjusting with one important twist. Instead of dividing, you multiply the U.S. dollar index (after you shift the decimal point two spaces to the right like you did with inflation-adjusting charts) by the appropriate future or cash product.

Let's start with a gold example. On July 31, 1993, gold closed at 407. The overwhelming technical consensus was on the August 2, 1993, cover of *Forbes*: "Next Stop in Gold: $500." Using the U.S. dollar index close to adjust gold to a real-world price, we get a currency-adjusted gold price of 392.06 for July 31, 1993 (407 × .9633). This was almost the same as the dollar-index-adjusted February 5, 1990, high of 425 (425 × .9220) and very close to a dollar-index-adjusted 25 percent retracement of the top off the January 21,1980, high (875 × .8570) and the low of September 2, 1992 (339.4 × .7841).

The U.S. dollar-index-adjusted gold chart makes you understand why gold's performance has been so puzzling to nominal chart technicians and why so many breakouts since August 1993 have not seen any follow-through. As you can see on Figure 12–4, currency-adjusted gold has been moving down along a

Figure 12–4

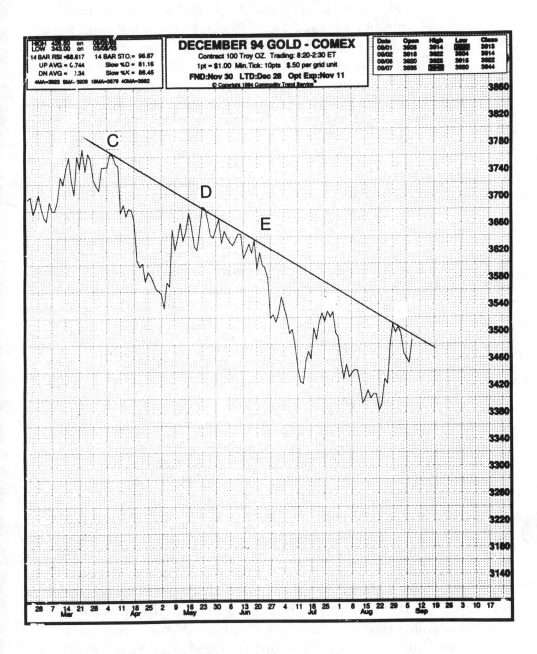

classic, almost 45-degree trendline.

At points A and B on Figures 12–4 and 12–5 both the nominal and currency-adjusted December gold chart followed the same path. But at point C, where the nominal price of December gold broke out, the currency-adjusted chart showed the trendline still intact. The same phenomena happened at points D and E.

Figure 12–6 shows a longer-term perspective on the weekly currency-adjusted gold chart. This chart was much more bearish than the nominal weekly gold chart (Figure 12–7). A classic strong right double-top was already in place when a nearly two-year trendline was broken on the currency-adjusted gold chart in late June of 1994.

No wonder the nominal price of gold followed the currency-adjusted chart technical breakdown by moving lower by nearly $20! The dollar is only a fraction of the total world currency situation. To the rest of the world, gold was looking lousy even though it looked like the long over due breakout here in the United States.

Crude's recent bottom and subsequent strength has been almost totally unexpected by techies (and the media, according to the February 28, 1994, *Forbes* cover). On December 17, 1993, front-month crude closed at 13.91, giving crude a currency-adjusted price of 13.31 (13.91 × .9567). On February 16, the currency-adjusted crude close was 13.26 (13.93 × .9516), and on March 10, it was 13.25 (14.14 × .9371). Any good technician would have recognized a classic strong right/lower close right double-bottom on the currency-adjusted crude chart. Wedded to nominal charts, most techies missed it.

Unfortunately, Figure 12–8, the currency-adjusted weekly crude chart, was plotted with weekly closes only, so the lower double-bottom of late winter in crude oil doesn't show up quite as well as it would on a daily, closest-to-cash, currency-adjusted crude chart. But this longer-term perspective does show clearly that the recent run-up in crude prices was not the breakout of the nominal charts (Figure 12–9, point A). On the currency-adjusted Figure 12–8, there is strong overhead resistance, a major

Figure 12-5

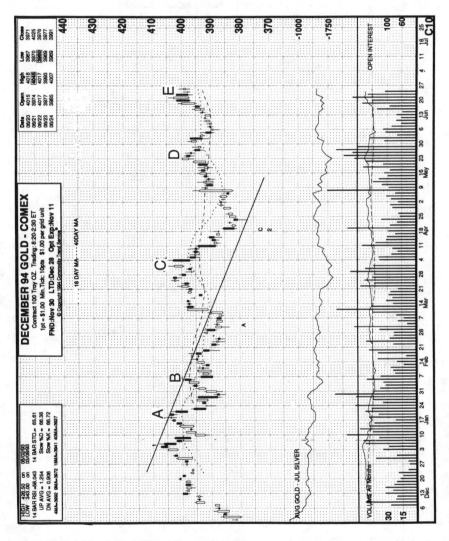

Figure 12–6

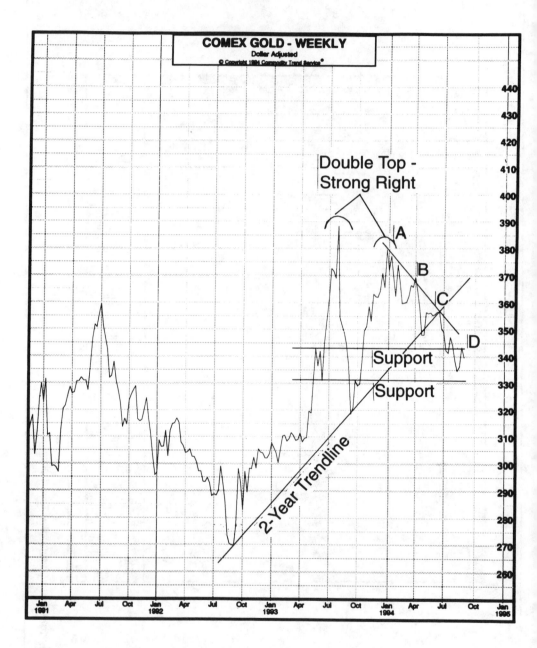

COMEX GOLD - WEEKLY
Dollar Adjusted
© Copyright 1994 Commodity Trend Service

Figure 12–7

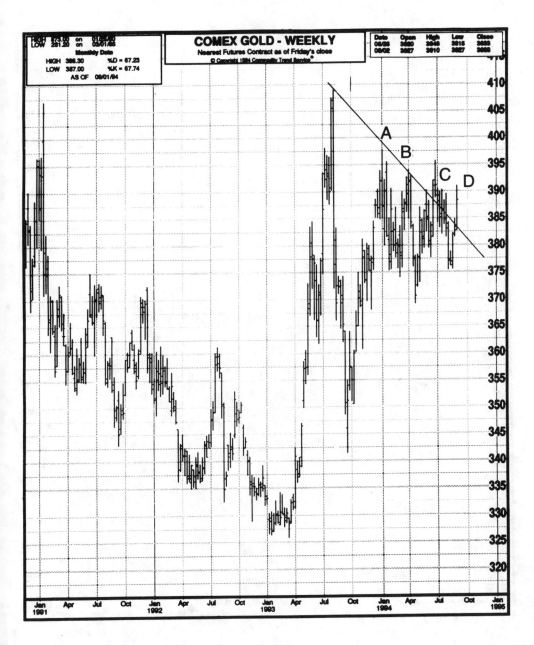

Figure 12-8

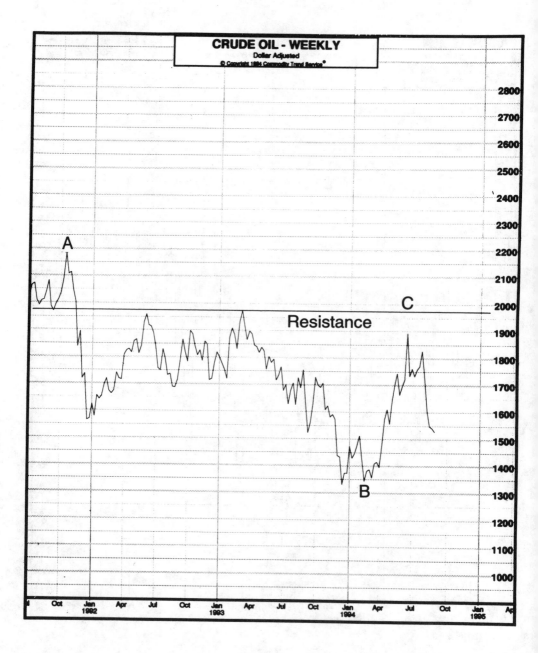

CRUDE OIL - WEEKLY
Dollar Adjusted
© Copyright 1994 Commodity Trend Service®

Figure 12-9

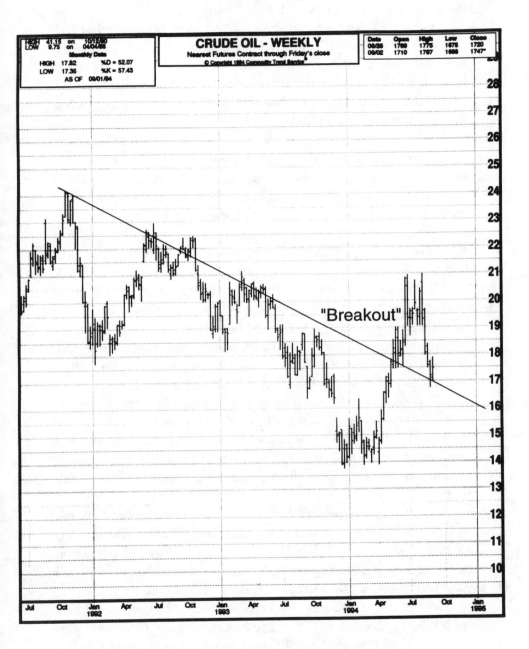

trendline that was never broken, and a 60 percent retracement (point C) from points A and B on Figure 12–8.

Figure 12–10 is a currency-adjusted chart of November soybeans. The new-crop beans were making a classic double-top before the recent price collapse. In addition, notice how this chart had a negative slant to the second double-top completely different to the breakout, ascending top pattern of the nominal November beans (Figure 12–11).

Figure 12–12, the currency-adjusted Dow, showed a perfect downtrend, until recently, that was even steeper than the downtrend in the nominal Dow (point A in both Figure 12-12 and Figure 12–13). But a strong right double-bottom and an upside breakout of the downtrend (point C) are one of the big reasons that the nominal Dow has showed surprising strength in August 1994. For the first time since January of 1994, the foreigners have had a reason to buy our stock market.

But as long as zone B in the currency-adjusted Dow (Figure 12–12) is not broken in a decisive way, it's unlikely we will move much higher in stocks. Just like gold a few months ago, it appears we are making a false breakout like we do so often on nominal charts. (In the next chapters, I will give you more reason why I feel the end is near for the 12-year bull run in stocks).

Figure 12–14 is the currency-adjusted corn chart plotted with weekly closes. Figure 12–15 is nominal weekly corn. Notice how on point A of the nominal chart, we have another short-lived breakout so common to trading in today's market. But point A in time on the currency-adjusted chart is perfectly on the trendline.

Point B is where corn bottomed and rallied in both charts. But notice how the currency-adjusted corn chart's bottom was so much easier to predict technically. The same phenomenon happened at Support Zone D in Figure 12–12. Corn bottomed exactly where classic technical theory would expect it—at the next logical support zone. Corn did bottom in the nominal charts (point B, Figure 12–15) in the general vicinity of where you would expect it to technically, but not with the exactness of the currency-adjusted charting.

Figure 12–10

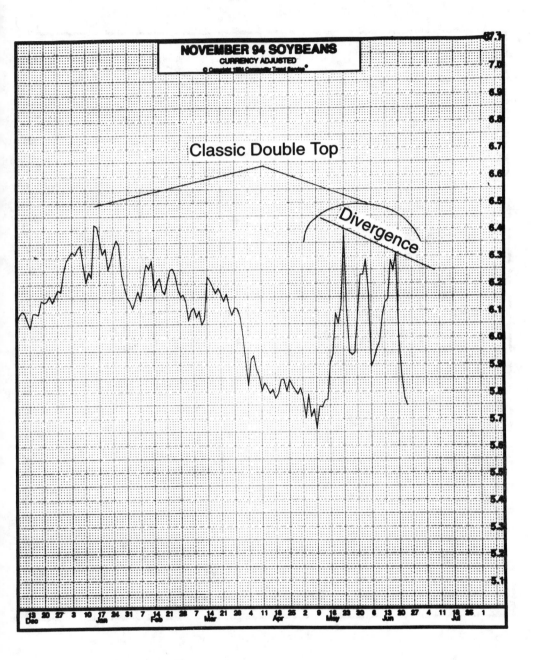

NOVEMBER 94 SOYBEANS
CURRENCY ADJUSTED

Classic Double Top

Divergence

Figure 12-11

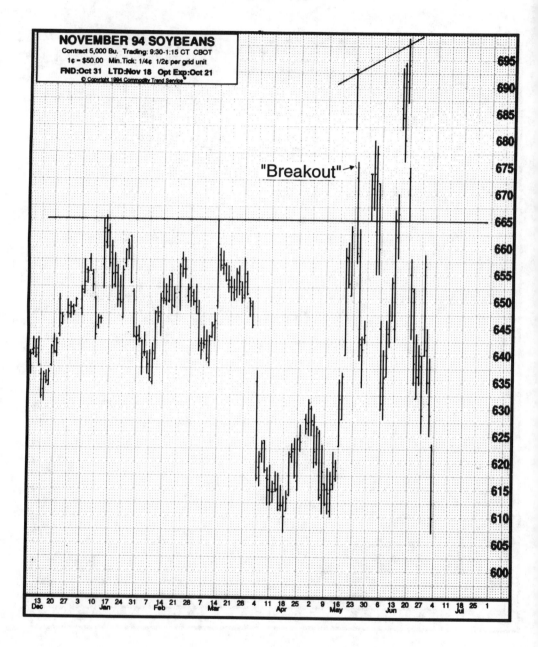

NOVEMBER 94 SOYBEANS
Contract 5,000 Bu. Trading: 9:30-1:15 CT CBOT
1¢ = $50.00 Min.Tick: 1/4¢ 1/2¢ per grid unit
FND:Oct 31 LTD:Nov 18 Opt Exp:Oct 21
© Copyright 1994 Commodity Trend Service

"Breakout"→

Figure 12–12

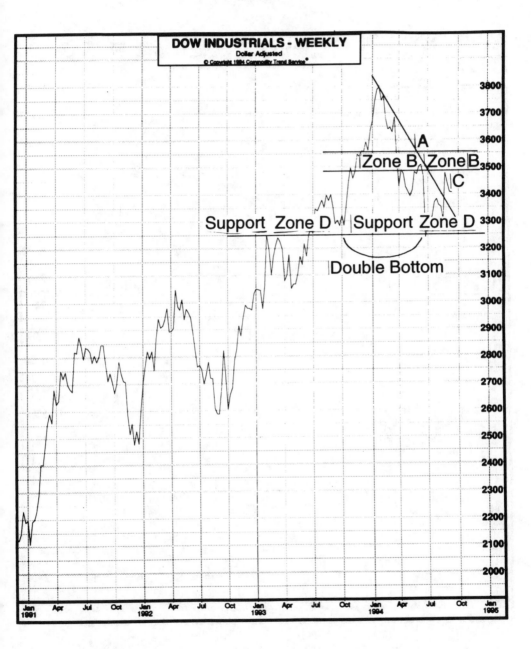

DOW INDUSTRIALS - WEEKLY
Dollar Adjusted
© Copyright 1994 Commodity Trend Service

Figure 12-13

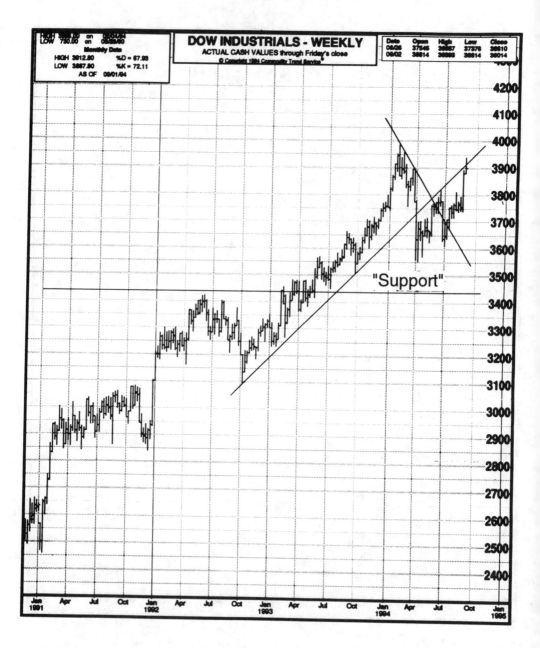

Figure 12-14

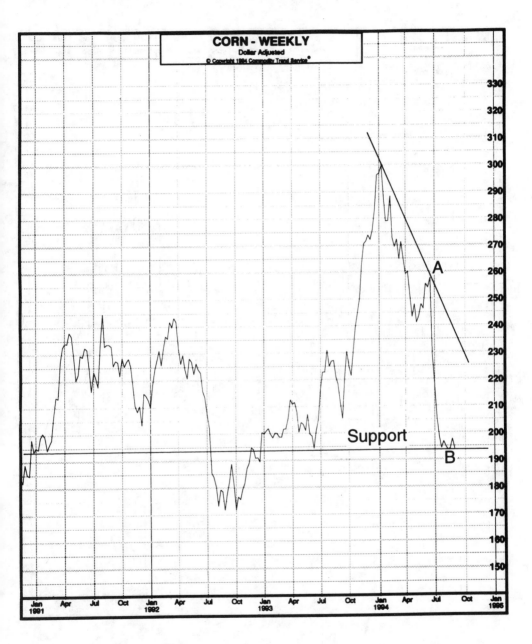

Figure 12-15

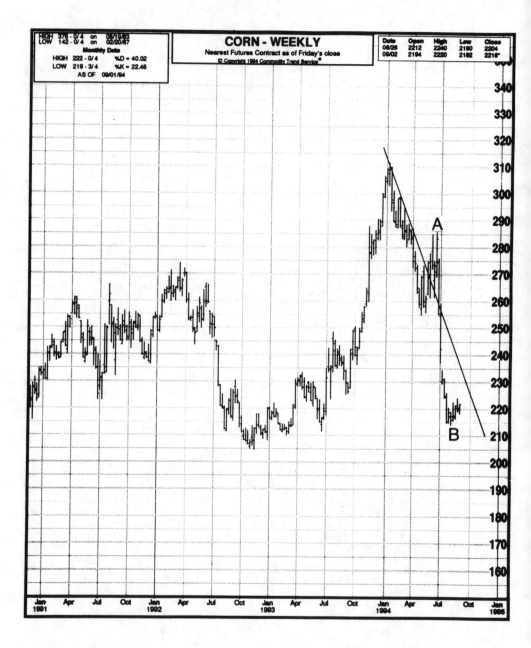

"The big money is at tops" is an old floor trader saying. Option premium, market movement, volume—they all peak at tops. But what does the technical trader say? "Don't pick tops or bottoms!" You can understand why the technical experts repeat this old saw when you see false breakouts and other mangled technical signals again and again at the tops and bottoms of the nominal chart. It's also why so many have gone into mechanical, price-based systems. If you can't pick tops and bottoms, you might as well be satisfied with getting the middle of the move from a trend-following system.

But when you combine currency-adjusted charts with other factors, like the media, you have a fighting chance to pick a top or a bottom. At virtually every one of the false breakouts I've pointed out on the nominal charts, the media was screaming "Buy! Buy!," which, as you will find out in a later chapter, means you should "Sell! Sell!" At tops and bottoms, you get so many techniques illustrated in this book saying the same thing, they resonate like the tolling of a church carillon.

There is a saying, "Nobody rings a bell to tell you the bull or bear market is over." But if you are using techniques like currency- and inflation-adjusted charts, techniques the herd barely considers, that bell may ring for you, like it does for so many professional traders.

Chapter Thirteen

Analogous Year

The great futures trader Roy Longstreet used to talk about finding an analogous year—a previous time in the market when circumstances were similar to those of the present. The idea is to use the comparison to help shed light on what might happen in the future. Many traders see nothing beyond their five-minute bar charts. But commercial firms employ people to do nothing but research the past to find parallels with today's markets. If you look hard enough, you can always find something in the past that seems to duplicate today's circumstances. Even the great inflation of the last fifty years has happened before (when massive imports of silver and gold from the New World inflated European economies in the sixteenth century).

Finding the Analogous Year

In the fall of 1993, I got a fax from my friend Jim Bianco. A household-name financial analyst was claiming that the stock market was repeating the early Kennedy years. And sure enough, there seemed to be a close relationship between stock market action following Kennedy's election and that following Clinton's election. Both were New Democrats that represented the start of a political generation, womanizers that were adored by the media after squeaking by their opponents—and, of course, there were the physical similarities that Clinton was careful to cultivate.

But right after I got Jim's fax, I called back and said, "He's not Kennedy, he's LBJ. It ain't 1962, it's 1966." After listening to my reasons, Jim quickly put together Figure 13–1. As you can see, the parallels between now and the 1960s stock market are incredible. Like Bush, Kennedy had a mixed record. He did cut taxes, but he also increased military spending and laid the foundation for the "guns-and-butter" fiasco of the LBJ administration, which set the stage for the stagflation that followed.

However, despite my discovery of the LBJ similarities (as revealed in Figure 13–1), the household-name analyst continued to promulgate the Kennedy-Clinton correspondence. His influence was apparent in the very bearish tone (versus the action) of the market in December 1993 and the first week of January 1994. Advisers were very cautious, considering the bull market had just reconfirmed the trend of the last decade with a renewed uptrend in the last quarter of 1993.

Even *Forbes* magazine got into the act. For the first time in my memory, their opening-year cover had a headline promising the lowdown on what stocks to short as well as the usual good buys of the year. In my opinion, this household-name analyst had helped to make it respectable to believe a stock top was near. If 1994 was going to be like 1962, the market would top the first week in January and have a horrible crash in April and May.

However, the first half of 1994 was almost a carbon copy of 1966, not 1962. When the expected top didn't come the first week of January, investors and the mainstream business media became giddy with delight, helping to create the February top. When the market sank in late March, investors thought, "Maybe it is 1962," and became far more bearish than they would otherwise normally have become after the first major pullback in over three years.

Figure 13-1

Kennedy/Johnson Stock Market versus Bush/Clinton Stock Market

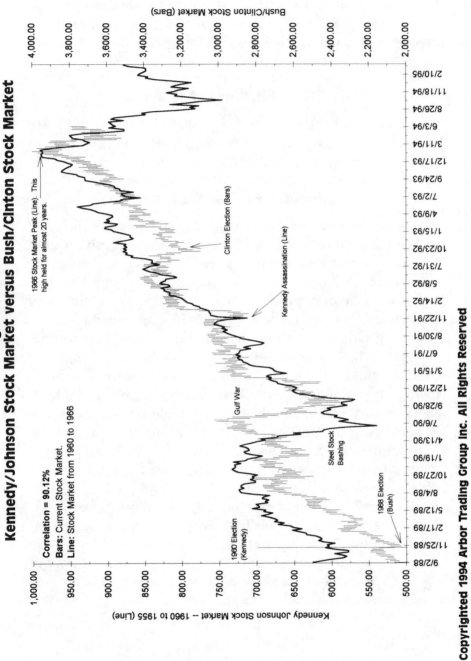

Correlation = 90.12%

Bars: Current Stock Market.
Line: Stock Market from 1960 to 1966

Which Year Is It Now?

As I write this late in the fall of 1994, it's obvious that the parallels with 1966 are beginning to break down. I think there are three possible factors that can help us find the next analogous year for future market action in stocks and bonds.

1994 Will Correct Itself

One possible factor is the expectation that 1994 has been a small period of deviation that will correct itself into the main pattern just like the summer of 1990 or the fall of 1993.

Clinton's Midterm Losses

Another factor was the growing realization by the stock and bond markets that Clinton would not be able to pass his massive health-care package and that Democrats are headed for disaster in the fall midterm elections. This perception picked up momentum in July when Clinton's press became increasingly negative, and commercials, like Jim Bianco of Arbor Trading, noted Clinton's continuing slide in voter approval, despite the good economy.

Figure 13–2 is a scattergraph by Jim Bianco of midterm election results of the incumbent party on the x-axis. The y-axis has the corresponding Gallup Poll approval numbers of a first-term president just before these midterm elections. Given Clinton's mid-August 1994 Gallup approval rating of 38 percent, the post-World-War-II history of the Gallup Poll would indicate the Democrats could experience a 44-seat massacre in the coming U.S. House elections!

In Figure 13-3, Jim Bianco has tracked Gallup approval and disapproval numbers for all first-term presidents since Eisenhower. Clinton is closely tracking Reagan. If the 1994 House Democrats lose the percentage of the 1982 Republicans, they will lose 13.54 percent of their seats: 37 seats from their 1992 total, or 35 seats if you subtract their recent two-seat loss in special elections.

Figure 13-2
Mid-Term Elections and Presidential Approval Ratings

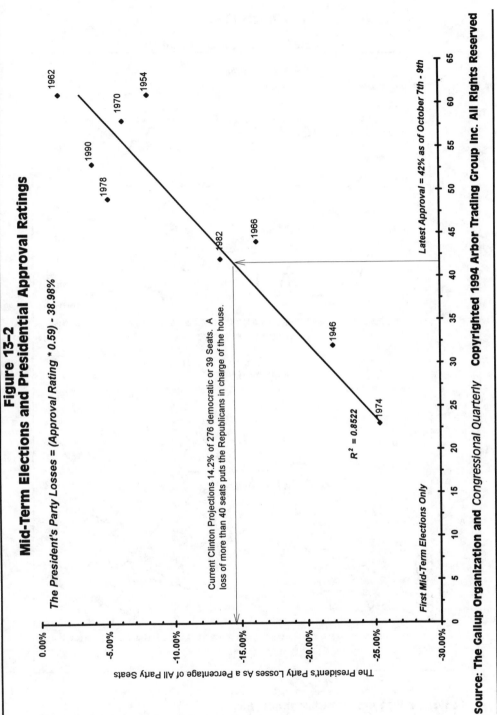

*The President's Party Losses = (Approval Rating * 0.59) - 38.98%*

Current Clinton Projections 14.2% of 276 democratic or 39 Seats. A loss of more than 40 seats puts the Republicans in charge of the house.

$R^2 = 0.8522$

Latest Approval = 42% as of October 7th - 9th

First Mid-Term Elections Only

The President's Party Losses As a Percentage of All Party Seats

Figure 13-3

How Does Clinton Stack Up

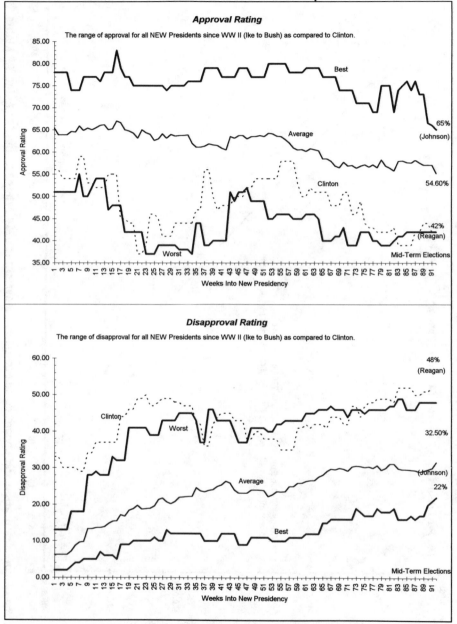

Approval Rating

The range of approval for all NEW Presidents since WW II (Ike to Bush) as compared to Clinton.

Disapproval Rating

The range of disapproval for all NEW Presidents since WW II (Ike to Bush) as compared to Clinton.

Copyright 1994 Arbor Trading Group, Inc.

Since 1946 there have been 12 midterm elections, which divide up into two groups of six each:

1. The disasters (average numeric House seat loss was 42, average percentage loss was 18.61 percent): 1946, 1950, 1958, 1966, 1974, and 1982.

2. Normal incumbent midterm losses (average loss 10 seats, average percentage loss 4.76 percent): 1954, 1962, 1970, 1978, 1986, and 1990.

The presidential approval Gallup Poll pattern of normal midterms is a slow decline that bottoms out a few months before the midterm election and then rises to a minor peak just before the midterm elections (note the Carter polls of 1977–1978).

The presidential poll numbers of midterm disasters follow this pattern—high at first, a big dip after six months, a rally, then back to the lows by midterm election time. Needless to say, Clinton's numbers (like Reagan's) are the classic midterm disaster pattern. High expectations are followed by big disappointments, then a second chance followed by total disillusionment and a furious "throw the bums out" mood for the midterm elections.

The question to come back to is how a large loss of Democratic House seats will affect the markets. How has this portending loss been causing the Dow to deviate from the 1960-1966 pattern since May of 1994? Because the stock and bond markets know something you were never taught in school: they understand the things I talked about in my mid-1993 report to clients called "Democrats: Bad for Bonds and Stocks."

Democrats: Bad for Bonds

Since 1861 (yearly data before 1901, monthly afterward) Republican presidents saw bond yields average a 4.94 percent decline versus a 12.93 percent rise under Democrats. Since 1913, the numbers are a 5.78 percent Republican decline versus a 15.66 percent Democratic rise. Since 1949, the gap has widened to a 4.86 percent Republican decline versus an astonishing 44.25 percent rise under Democrat—graphic evidence that Democratic politicians have become more and more liberal, anti-business, and inflationary as this century has progressed.

Since 1913, the average low in yields under Republican administrations has been 22.5 months after they start. Under Democratic administrations, it has been 7.25 months. Almost all gains in bond yields under Democrats come in the second half of their administrations. Bond yields rise even faster after big midterm Democratic losses (which I expect in 1994). After the 1938 and 1946 elections, bond yields rose sharply despite strong yield downtrends before these elections. After the 1966 and 1978 defeats, bond rates soared to record levels.

The history of Democratic administrations says the lowest bond yields of the Clinton administration will have been early September 1993, then an increase of 44 percent by June 1997, or to an 8.3 percent yield (if the recent 5.75 percent bottom holds). Republicans in trouble (like Bush or Ford) continue policies that lower interest rates. Democrats in trouble (Truman, LBJ, Carter) spend more and pump up the money supply. It is quite normal for bond yields to go down in the first year of a Democratic administration. Average monthly yields went down 6.7 percent or more during the first year of Wilson, FDR, Truman, and JFK. Even LBJ's first year saw a slight downtick in bond yields. But eventually the new Democratic policies overwhelm the anti-inflation stance of previous Republican administrations.

Democrats Increase Government's Share of GDP

In the 1980s, even Sweden cut the percentage of GDP accounted for by government spending (from 65 percent to 60 percent). The U.S. federal government's percentage of GDP went from 25.4 percent in 1982 to 23 percent in 1989. This small but significant rollback in the share the government accounts for in the world economy is a big reason for the great bond bull market of the 1980s.

Big government suppresses economic growth, which increases strains on the debt market. Rising government expenditures and regulations are only noninflationary under wartime controls or depressions. There is a direct relationship between less government and low inflation. It's no accident that Japan, with the lowest percentage of GDP used by the government (32.8 percent) of any major nation also has the lowest inflation rate.

The recent increase of the federal government's share in the U.S. economy from 23 percent to 25.4 percent of GDP has been funded because U.S. banks have shifted from their traditional lending activities to buying government securities. The slow-down in economic growth has resulted in fewer borrowers over-all; those who are trying to borrow tend to be of a lower credit quality. Since March 1989, banks have increased their holdings of government securities by about $300 billion while reducing their business loans outstanding by around $15 billion. This process has already hurt government revenues and ballooned the deficit. It can't continue much longer.

Democrats Increase Taxes

Increasing taxes also has a long-term effect of increasing inflation and bond rates because higher taxes raise costs and justify bigger government spending. Tax increases (direct or bracket creep) under Theodore Roosevelt, Wilson, Hoover, Eisenhower, LBJ, Nixon, and Carter led to higher interest rates. Decreasing taxes after the Civil War, under Coolidge, during the early years of FDR (the end of deflation increased the ability to pay taxes), under Truman (by cutting tariffs and war time taxes), and under Reagan led to lower interest rates.

It's worth noting the average monthly bond yields of January 1960 (4.42 percent) were only exceeded in January 1966, six years later. The anti-inflationary effect of JFK's tax decreases was eventually overwhelmed by LBJ's guns-and-butter policy—just as the (relatively) small Bush tax increase did not prevent lower interest rates when the banking system was radically shifted from lending to buying government securities. But as LBJ's policies overwhelmed the policies of Eisenhower and Kennedy, Bush and Clinton are putting a one-two knockout punch to Reagan's anti-tax, anti-government, anti-inflation policies. Clinton is another liberal Democrat who will increase taxes, spending, and government regulations (see Figure 13-4)—which, in turn, will increase inflation and interest rates.

Democrats: Also Bad for Stocks

While many people will agree that Democrats are bad for bonds, many investors think Democrats are good (or at least not bad) for stocks. Actually stocks have rallied during only three out of the 11 Democratic presidential administrations since 1892: Truman's anemic 10 percent, Kennedy's very atypical tax-cut administration, and FDR's first term when stocks recovered after losing nearly 90 percent from 1929-1932. Leaving aside FDR's first term as a fluke, four out of the seven Democratic presidents since 1892 (Cleveland, Wilson, FDR, and Carter) have seen the market crash by 25 percent or greater during their terms in office. By contrast, eight out of the 11 Republican presidential terms since 1896 saw stocks rise. Five out of the 11 Republican presidents (Theodore Roosevelt, Harding, Coolidge, Eisenhower, and Reagan) saw gains in the Dow of at least 100 percent.

Except for Carter in 1978, every new Democratic president has seen the stock market go up after their election for a little more than a year, and then crash. From Wilson to LBJ, this has been the pattern:

1. A median rally of 29.83 percent over 15.4 months. Measured from the October 1992 low made after the first debate (when Clinton appeared to be a sure winner), that would give us a closing-Dow top in February 1994 of around 4072.

2. The subsequent crash has averaged a 26.88 percent decline over seven months. Often this is only the first leg of a multiyear bear market.

I believe Carter was the only twentieth-century aberration because Nixon was the only Republican (other than Hoover) to govern like a Democrat—out-of-control spending and regula-

Figure 13–4
Is Increased Governmental Control Inflationary?

Correlation = .94

In 1993, the Federal Register rose by 10.76% over 1992 to 69,688 pages. This is well above its post World War 2 average of 4.55% Through June 9, 1994, the Federal Register is on pace for a 68,900 pages year.

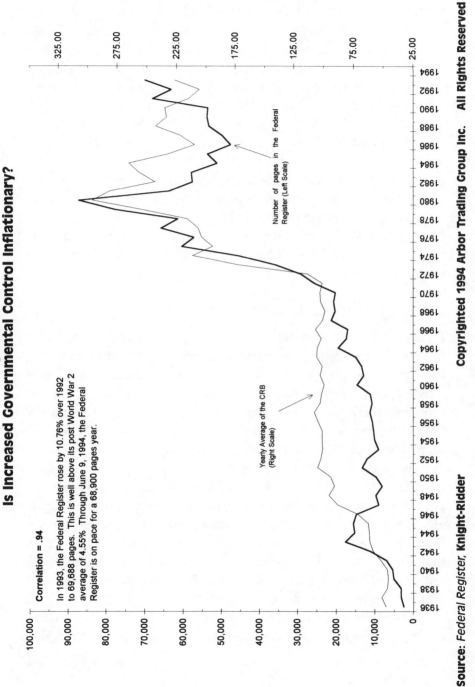

Number of pages in the Federal Register (Left Scale)

Yearly Average of the CRB (Right Scale)

tions, price controls, etc. Carter inherited a wrecked economy which he promptly made worse—therefore, no first-year stock rally. Bush might have been economically unsophisticated, but his policies, unlike Nixon's, were deflationary. Clinton at least inherited an economy that was (just barely) stable and rising.

Skipping the war years, the Democrats have had six midterm elections this century where they suffered losses (1918, 1938, 1946, 1950, 1966, and 1978). Using these six times as data, the Dow has rallied from a median bottom of the July before the midterm election to a median top in November 14.29 percent above the July bottom (4050 Dow level and of 1994). The Dow then declines a median 13.15 percent by February of the next year, as the market euphoria is replaced with the reality that a liberal Democratic president is going to veto any changes initiated by Republicans or a Republican/conservative-Democratic coalition in Congress.

Regulation Is Inflationary

Figure 13-4 is the correlation between inflation and the number of pages in the Federal Register. It is very important to note that the history of post-World-War-II Democratic presidents is that they respond to electoral pressure by promoting even more government: there were more pages in the Federal Register in 1948 than 1946, more in 1952 than 1950, more in 1968 than in 1966, and many more in 1979–1980 than in 1978. This is what makes the portending Democratic midterm losses so dangerous. In fact, only once since 1948—in Ronald Reagan's first term—have we seen the pages of the Federal Register go down from a midterm election to the next presidential election. Increasing federal regulation is an almost irresistible electoral triple play—a chance to look like you are doing something for the public at the same time you reward (and shake down for contributions) the special interests that will support your reelection.

Since the start of 1991, there has been a big jump in the number of pages of the Federal Register. By the end of 1993, the

U.S. economy had experienced two big tax increases and seen the number of pages in the Federal Register jump over 33 percent in the last three years. This has only happened twice in the last 50 years: during World War II, and in the 1970s when bracket creep constantly raised the real rate of taxes. Both times resulted in horrendous inflation and a big swoon in both the stock and bond markets.

The New Analogous Year Is 1973

I believe the 1960–1966 analogy in the stock market has broken down because the new analogous year is now 1973. Like the fall of 1973, the economy is beginning to run into capacity limits thanks to loose monetary policy not being counterbalanced with correct fiscal policy (like the Kennedy and Reagan tax cuts, or the slow growth of government during the Reagan and Eisenhower years).

Investors Are Tapped Out

The top of Figure 13–5 shows the ratio of equity funds (stock mutual funds) as a percentage of the stock market. It shows that the public is up to its eyeballs in stocks. If the foreigners are reluctant to buy (thanks to our weak dollar), if pension funds are putting in their maximum amount of contributions thanks to a booming economy, and individuals are maxed out, who's left to buy stocks? The lower half of this figure shows how little cash is left in this economy. Whenever cash has gotten this low, stocks have taken a big tumble (1962, 1970, 1981–1982).

The Deficit and National Bankruptcy

As for bonds, consider this comment from the August 29, 1994, issue of *National Review*, p.19:

> The interest-rate risk was recently quantified by Richard George, a financial analyst and editor of the *The Derivative Risk Analyst*. According to Mr. George's

Figure 13-5

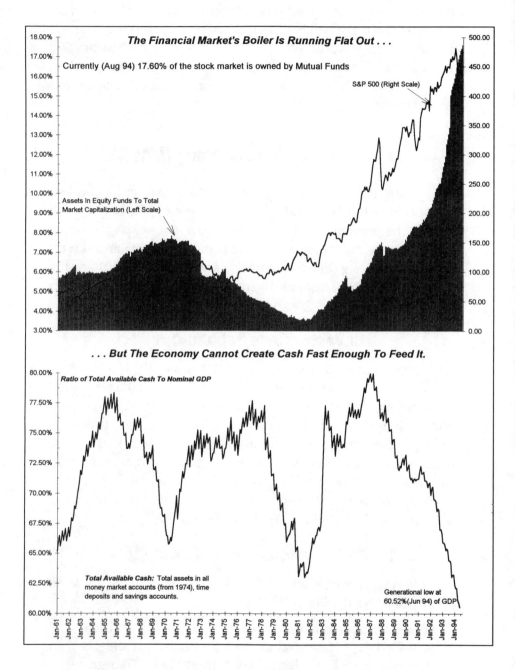

The Financial Market's Boiler Is Running Flat Out . . .

Currently (Aug 94) 17.60% of the stock market is owned by Mutual Funds

S&P 500 (Right Scale)

Assets In Equity Funds To Total Market Capitalization (Left Scale)

. . . But The Economy Cannot Create Cash Fast Enough To Feed It.

Ratio of Total Available Cash To Nominal GDP

Total Available Cash: Total assets in all money market accounts (from 1974), time deposits and savings accounts.

Generational low at 60.52%(Jun 94) of GDP

Source: The Gallup Organization, Arbor Trading Group, Inc.

model, a sustained interest-rate rise of as little as 365 basis points (3.65 percent) would send the deficit sky-rocketing to $600 billion by 1998. At that point interest on the federal debt would equal personal income taxes. Private investors would probably refuse to buy additional Treasury bonds. If you add in a mild recession and a slightly lower revenue assumption (19 percent of GDP instead of 19.7 percent assumed by the CBO), the day of reckoning moves up to 1996, and the interest-rate trigger drops to 275 basis points.

Since 1969, the federal deficit cycle has been moving higher and higher: every recovery low in the deficit is higher than the last economic peak, every recession high in the deficit is much higher than the previous record in the last recession. Each new recovery low or recession high has been greater than the last one by a ratio of approximately 3- or 4-to-1. For example, during the inflationary boom of the late 1970s, the deficit came down to only around $50 billion, only to balloon to over $200 billion in the 1982 recession. After Reagan whittled this down to around $100 billion despite howls from the liberals and their media henchmen, the next recession under Bush saw the deficit sky-rocket to $350 billion. If this trend continues, we will see the deficit bloat to approximately $600 billion in the next recession—if only we make the rather safe assumption that the federal deficit will never get below $150 billion during the current "economic recovery."

Facing national bankruptcy if they let the economy go into recession, the Federal Reserve is going to be under enormous pressure to inflate at all cost. In any case, if the first two appointments he made are indicators, very soon Clinton will succeed in filling the Fed with inflation-oriented appointees. The new Fed Vice Chairman, Alan Blinder, heir apparent to Greenspan, has already publicly criticized his colleagues for being too worried about inflation and not worried enough about economic growth. If reelection politics come before any monetary stability, we will return to Carternomics or Nixonomics and inflation will go wild.

The Dollar and Grain Prices
over the Next Few Years

There is one last reason to back up the assumption that we are entering (if we haven't already entered) a period like 1973–1974. Republicans are not above debasing the dollar (1985–1987 under Reagan, 1969–1973 under Nixon), but it's worth noting there has been no peacetime Democratic administration in this century that has raised the value of the dollar. Democrats are as bad for the dollar as they are for stocks and bonds. As James Carville, Clinton's political adviser said, "I looove the stock market falling. In the 1980s the stock market rose 300 percent and real incomes fell. Maybe now the stock market will fall and real incomes will rise."

Over the last 25 years we have had three great debasements of the dollar: 1969–1973, 1977–1978, and 1986–1987. Each was followed by higher commodity prices and falling bonds and stocks. Even the mini-collapse of 1989-1990 in the dollar was followed by a mini-collapse in bonds and stocks and an uptick in the CRB. In 1994, the dollar plunged to its lowest levels against the yen since World War II.

According to Jim Bianco, the CRB index has an .83 correlation to bond yields. Since the CRB is about 40 percent in grains, many have criticized it for being too agricultural to be useful as an inflation gauge. But according to Bianco, other indexes like the Goldman Sachs Commodity Index (GSCI) are far less correlated to bonds (.43 for the GSCI).

While we in the U.S. spend only 20–25 percent of our total income on food, this percentage is far higher in the rest of the world. You can turn down the thermostat and even move to a cheaper lodging, but there is only so much you can do to scrimp on food. Skyrocketing food prices divert sums that would have been invested, shunting off funds that could buy bonds or stocks.

There are five reasons to expect at least a 50 percent increase in the price of grains over the next two years:

1. Presidential politics in an election year always have an effect on prices.

Only about 5 percent of the U.S. population is directly involved in agriculture, but farmers and people who depend on them have a political clout well beyond their numbers. Farmers are more likely to vote and contribute to political candidates. They disproportionately live in states that are going to be critical for Clinton's reelection: Illinois, Ohio, Missouri, Iowa, and Wisconsin. Farm states like South Dakota, North Dakota, and Montana may have only .75 percent of the population of the U.S. but they have (thanks to their two senators) 1.67 percent of the total percentage of the electoral college.

Since 1936, grain prices have suffered big declines only twice during a presidential year: 1968 and 1992. It's no accident that the incumbent lost both times in a close race. You can be sure that Clinton knows that fact. The presidential effect has seen corn gain about 20 percent (15 percent median gain) from the harvest low of the year before the presidential election (1991) to the time of the election itself. One calendar year after the presidential election, corn prices have declined 5 percent on average.

2. U.S. agricultural prices are at an all-time low.

In July 1991, the closest-to-cash corn future reached 2.23, beans 5.14, wheat 2.50, and oats 1.035 a bushel. After inflation, these prices are far lower than the Depression lows of 1932, and even lower than the 1842 lows. They were the lowest agricultural prices in U.S. history. Three years later in July of 1994, corn was at 2.14, beans at 5.7125, wheat 3.04, and oats 1.095. Since inflation has gone up 8.95 percent since then, the equivalent prices today for the July 1991 prices would be corn 2.43, beans 5.60 (beans got below this price in the new-crop November beans), wheat 2.72, and oats 1.1275. As you can see, in 1994 some grains were higher than three years prior, some lower than in 1991 after inflation adjusting. I think we can safely say that we are making a classic long-term double-bottom in U.S. grain prices.

Double-tops and double-bottoms are quite common on long-term inflation-adjusted charts. They almost always indicate a major trend change is near. When beans reached 12.90 a bushel in June 1973, it was almost exactly the same price, after inflation, of their 3.90 price top in the fall of 1917. When crude oil reached 40 a barrel in 1979, it was very close to the inflation-adjusted highs reached during the Civil War. The double-bottom in grain prices is almost surely a sign of much higher grain prices to come.

3. A record year in corn production is almost always followed by a bad year.

Since 1900, a new-record corn yield has been set 25 times, better than once every four years. We had another record corn yield in 1994. There is a very strong pattern of price recovery after record years in corn (see Table 13-1):

Table 13-1

Record Yield Year	*Approx. Rise One to Two Years from*
Harvest Low	
1987	150 %
1982	75 %
1979	50 %
1969	40 %
Record Production Year	
1973	60 %
1967	35 %
1963	20 %
1960	20 %
1946	125 %
1906	100 %

Back-to-back record years are almost unheard of in grain production.

4. El Niño is finally going to arrive next year.

In early 1992, I remember seeing a banner hanging over the

agricultural trading floor of the Board of Trade: "El Niño is Coming." The talk of the whole industry (including the financial press) was how El Niño was going to drive grain prices to the roof that year. Needless to say, the very time the business media did features on El Niño (January–February 1992) was the top of the corn market for a long time to come.

In July 1991, Mount Pinatubo erupted in the Philippines. Some called it the most cataclysmic event that has occurred on earth in well over 150 years. Fine ash shot up over 100,000 feet, with an estimated 80 million tons of sulfur dioxide sent into the atmosphere. These volcanic aerosols reflect sunlight back into space. The eruption of low-latitude volcanos restricts the amount of sunlight that reaches the earth near the equator. Less energy means a reduction of the trade winds and a profound change in Pacific currents. Surface water is no longer replaced by cooler water. The resulting warming effect, or El Niño, can have profound weather consequences.

For example, the El Niño of 1976–1977 generated a Brazilian coffee freeze and a bull market due to drought in cocoa. There was also a mild drought that sent corn and bean prices upward. The 1982–1983 El Niño saw another Brazilian coffee freeze, record floods in California, and drought in various areas from the cocoa regions of Africa to the U.S. Midwest. The 1986–1987 El Niño damaged wheat crops around the world. The Mount Pinatubo eruption was the largest since Tambora erupted in 1815. After that eruption, 1816 was called "the year without a summer" in New England. In 1818, three years after the Tambora eruption, Ohio experienced a freeze that killed all the corn in the state. You can see why El Niño was quite a topic in the grain pit after Pinatubo erupted. However, a mild El Niño merely causes a slight cooling that increases rainfall in the Midwest. Such has been the effect of Pinatubo over the last three years.

Now that the "El Niño is coming" banner over the grain pits has been long forgotten, it is time to remember that the ash of a major volcano can lie in the air for up to seven years and the sulfuric acid it generates peaks three years after the event. We are merely reaching the peak of the effects of Pinatubo. Over the last few years, the only El Niño effect has been 1994's freakish weather (record cold, record low rainfall for some months in some areas) and the record rainfall and floods of 1993. Just the slightest change in weather—for example, if the drought we had in April and May 1994 had occurred in June and July 1994 instead—will send prices into orbit from very depressed levels. (The severe freeze in the coffee-growing regions of Brazil was a very good sign that the intensity of El Niño is increasing.)

5. It's time for a big grain rise.

In this century, 24 times corn prices have advanced over 50 percent from the harvest low of one year to a peak one year later; that's about once very four years. The last big one—a large rise in grain prices—was in 1988. We are due for one in 1994 or 1995 (more on the cyclic reasons for this in the next chapter).

Grain price increases of 100–200 percent or greater in the space of two years or less have occurred quite often in twentieth-century grain prices (see Table 13-2).

Table 13-2

Beans	1932–1934:	45 cents to $1.50
	1936–1937:	25 cents to $1.80
	1946–1948:	$2.20 to $4.45
	1971–1973:	$2.97-3/4 to $12.90
	1986–1988:	$4.67-1/2 to $10.99-1/2
Corn	1916–1917:	60 cents to $2.35
	1933–1935:	22 cents to $1.10
	1946–1947:	$1.10 to $2.97
	1972–1974:	$1.18-3/4 to $4.00
	1986–1988:	$1.49-1/4 to $3.59
Wheat	1916–1917:	$1.00 to $3.45
	1933 :	45 cents to $1.15
	1946–1947:	$1.60 to $3.20

Table 13-2 (continued)

	1972–1974:	$1.40 to $6.45
	1977–1979:	$2.14-1/2 to $4.86
Oats	1901–1902:	22 cents to 70 cents
	1916–1918:	35 cents to 92 cents
	1933–1935:	60 cents to $1.16
	1946–1947:	75 cents to $1.53-1/2
	1972–1974:	65 cents to $2.03
	1986–1988:	93 cents to $3.93

I may have missed one or two other 100+ percent moves in grains. However, the point is, which is more likely? The Dow doubling to 8,000 or corn doubling to 4.40? Bonds making a 50 percent rise in value or corn prices going up 50 percent to 3.30? We may not get a once-in-a-lifetime explosion like the 400 percent increase in soybean prices from 1972–1974. But the potential is there. Even a standard, once-in-about-four-years 50 percent increase will make many fortunes over the next few years for people not locked into stocks and bonds. One thing you should keep in mind: although in general inflation is not good for the economy (and I have spent a great deal of time explaining the damage Democratic inflation-oriented policies have wrought on the economy), there is nothing like an exploding market to create the opportunity for traders to get rich. In general, traders love volatility and large price moves, whether inflation-induced or not.

Even if I am wrong and this is not 1973, but a continuation of the 1960s in stocks, bonds, and futures, you should remember that the Dow topped in real terms in 1966 and has not been higher since. Gold is not $35 an ounce and corn has never seen $1.00 a bushel again. We may be on the verge of a gigantic shift away from financial assets into paying debts and buying food at ever-higher prices (this is one of the reasons why I feel gold will not explode in price right away with a falling bond and stock market).

Like every other technique, you can't use Analogous Year methods to the exclusion of all other techniques. But if you don't study the past you may get trapped in a losing position that never gave you a good reversal warning in the charts or with any other technical indicator. It's one more technique you can add to determine a top or bottom—the areas of trading that have the most risk but also most of the profit potential.

Chapter Fourteen

Long-Term Cycles

In the July/August 1992 issue of *Cycles* magazine, I wrote an article, "The Blowout Stock Top of 1993: Megacycles and the U.S. Election." It was quite an opus—chockful of cycles of all sorts. Several readers called to congratulate me on my work.

I should have known after those congratulatory calls I was on the wrong track. After all, no reader of *Futures* magazine called me about "1987 Was Not 1929," their June 1988 summary of a report I sent to my clients in early 1988. The prospects of a potential trade are usually inversely proportional to how many other people like it. That certainly was the case when I was a broker. And it was definitely true for this *Cycles* article: "Stocks likely will have an enormous advance until mid-1993, partly because of a surprising Republican showing in Congress. Late 1993 should see a stock and economic collapse, with rising prices and interest rates." I guess you would call these statements from my article good prognostication only if you considered a 20 percent rise in the Dow an "enormous advance."

The "king" of cycles, Edward M. Dewey, predicted in his 1947 book *Cycles* (New York: Hawthorn) that "on the basis of past performance, four major rhythms declining together can possibly make a very deep economic depression indeed, starting with a crest of 'good times' in 1946 or 1947, and working downward to the bottom of the trough in perhaps 1951 or 1952." By the end of his life, Dewey, despite all his immense research as the head of the Foundation for the Study of Cycles, had wisely stopped making predictions based on cycles.

But just like Analogous Year, using cycles is much better than flying blind and depending on some oscillator or chart to guide you through the tops and bottoms of turbulent markets. So with some trepidation and a lot of humility in my own ability to find effect cycles, I offer the following observations.

The 55.5-Year Long-Wave Cycle

In 1922, A.C. Tchijevsky published "The Investigation of the Relationship Between Sunspot Activity and the Course of the Universal Historical from the Fifth Century B.C. to the Present Day." Tchijevsky studied the events of 2,400 years of human history and constructed a human excitability index using this data.

The peaks of this human excitability index showed a strong 11.1-year cycle, which is the dominant (but by no means the only) cycle in sunspots. Tchijevsky, in a leap typical of cycle experts, concluded that sunspots were causing these peaks. The only problem was that the highs of his index occurred one year behind the highs of sunspot activities.

Another Russian Marxist of the 1920s, Kondratieff, proposed the infamous Kondratieff Wave. Using only 200 years of wholesale prices, Kondratieff proposed an economic long-wave cycle of around 54 years. The popular version of the Kondratieff went something like this:

1. A strong period of growth finished off by a war:
    Cycle 1A: War of 1812
    Cycle 2A: Civil War
    Cycle 3A: World War I
    Cycle 4A: Vietnam War

2. A peak in the purchasing power of commodities:
   Cycle 1B: 1814
   Cycle 2B: 1864
   Cycle 3B: 1920
   Cycle 4B: 1973

3. A sharp recession after the commodity peak:
   Cycle 1C: 1815
   Cycle 2C: 1866
   Cycle 3C: 1921
   Cycle 4C: 1975

4. A recovery or plateau period which ends in a speculative blow-off:
   Cycle 1D: 1814–1818 (4 years)
   Cycle 2D: 1866–1873 (7 years)
   Cycle 3D: 1921–1929 (8 years)
   Cycle 4D: 1976–1989 (8–13 years)

5. A period of depression and/or deflation:
   Cycle 1E: 1819–1843
   Cycle 2E: 1873–1899
   Cycle 3E: 1929–1949
   Cycle 4E: ?

Each crest had a major political scandal, a real-estate boom, and a women's rights movement. All in all, during the late 1970s and early 1980s it was easy to sell the gloomy conclusion that the forces of economic history were pointing inevitably toward a new depression.

I believe the best of cycle theory is combined in the hypothetical 11.1-year economic cycle I proposed in a March 1987 article, as shown in Table 14-1:

Table 14-1
Hypothetical 11.1-Year Economic Cycle

Bottom of Depression	Start of Prosperity	Start of Rapid Growth	Commodity Top	Speculative Top
1496.36	1507.47	1518.58	1529.69	1540.80
1551.91	1563.02	1574.13	1585.24	1596.35
1607.46	1618.57	1629.68	1640.79	1651.90
1663.01	1674.12	1685.23	1696.34	1707.45
1718.56	1729.67	1740.78	1751.89	1763.00
1774.11	1785.22	1796.33	1807.04	1818.55
1829.66	1840.77	1851.88	1862.99	1874.10
1885.21	1896.32	1907.43	1918.54	1929.54
1940.76	1951.87	1962.98	1974.09	1985.20
1996.31?				

When you study the dominant economies of each era (sixteenth-century Italy; France and Holland in the seventeenth century; eighteenth- and nineteenth-century England; and the United States in the twentieth century), you find this proposed cycle chart has a remarkable historical fit. To cite just one example, the highest three years of unemployment in nineteenth-century England were 1884 through 1886.

Kondratieff's famous cycle was based on only four repetitions. The 11.1-year economic cycle shown in Table 14-1 can be traced historically through nine repetitions. But we can extend this 55-year cycle back 13 repetitions by using wheat prices. Interest rates seem to move together in an inverse 55-year cycle relationship with wheat (high real wheat prices, low real interest rates, low real wheat prices, high real interest rates). We have wheat prices back to 1281 and can trace this 55-year wheat cycle back another four cycles. Inflation-adjusted wheat prices in 1994 came near the record lows reached in 1991. Given all we know about the present world economic situation, would anyone want to bet their long-term economic future that real interest rates won't peak in 1996-1997 and start the fourteenth repetition of the 55-year cycle since 1281?

There are four "coincidences" over the last 500 years that have occurred in all the years following the "Speculative Top":

1. A worldwide decline in wealth (the worldwide bull markets in stocks and bonds have been more than counterbalanced by the collapse of such dollar-denominated assets as gold, crude oil, Eurodollars, U.S. real estate, and securities together with the 50 percent collapse in the Japanese stock prices and the beginning of the unraveling of Japanese real estate). I proposed this cycle in spring of 1987. At the height of the U.S. stock boom, did anything else predict that the world economy stood on the verge of a global slowdown that would affect even Germany and Japan? Even the latest stock rally could have been predicted by this cycle. U.S. stocks seem to have a last-gasp rally seven to eight years after the speculative top (1826, 1881, 1937, and now 1993).

2. The highest real interest rates of the last 50 years, leading to a worldwide depression (previous eras, I concede, have not always been as bad as the 1930s).

3. Enormous political upheaval, such as the recent ruling-party debacles, are just the start of remarkable changes in this cycle.

4. The hottest economy before the Speculative Top becomes the worst economy during the depression. That was the United States in the 1930s. In the 1990s, I believe Japan's real estate and stock markets will lead the way down, despite this year's feeble rally in Japanese stocks.

Human nature never changes. One generation grows up seeing the consequences of too much debt (Depression generation). They run their businesses prudently. But their children see only prosperity. (The prosperity generation of today are the baby boomers like Clinton. In the 1920s, they were called the jazz-age generation). These children borrow and speculate up to the hilt because they think prosperity is forever.

Eventually the bubble bursts. (In 1929 it was a stock crash. Today I believe we will see a collapse in the bond market.) The whole debt mountain comes down like a ton of bricks. *Each depression is worse than the last because the debt mountain is piled higher in terms of the expanding nature of fiat money.*

Bill Clinton is the political wonderchild of his age. He believes his economic policies will ensure prosperity continues forever, and his answer is more government. Clinton will continue to borrow, tax, and manipulate, oblivious to the need to ease the governmental burden on Joe Average who is staggering under a massive load of private and public debt.

Gold and Bonds after the Speculative Top

If you ask the average investor what does well in depressions, he would reply, government bonds and gold. Leaving aside the very pertinent question of whether the U.S. government can pay its bills over the long term, this answer is still not quite true. Those who held gold and U.S. bonds throughout the Great Depression did well. But during the early part of the crisis, gold fell from a yearly average price of 20.67 an ounce in 1928 to 17.06 in 1931. U.S. bonds fell 20 percent from January 1931 to July 1932. Baa-rated bonds went from an average yield of 7.5 percent in August 1931 to 11.6 percent six months later. From the middle of 1931 to the middle of 1932, railroad bonds lost 36 percent, foreign bonds 45 percent, and many issues lost even more.

As far as I can tell (records are pretty scanty before 1700), this phenomenon has always happened near the start of the period between the Speculative Top and the Depression Bottom. Here are two examples:

* English bonds had a big fall from 1818 to 1820, while gold fell in English commodity terms over 11 percent from 1820 to 1825. There was also a sharp fall in the dollar price of gold during this period.

* According to Warren and Pearson's classic study[1] of the history of prices, gold in English commodity terms fell 20 percent from 1878 to 1882, only to climb 80 percent in commodity terms over the next decade and a half.

* U.S. bonds fell from 1874 to 1879, only to rebound strongly over the next two decades.

History says that falling gold and bond prices often accompany the start of hard times as investors attempt to pay off debts and prop up their businesses by liquidating assets. As the depression gathers strength despite this liquidation, panic sets in and people begin to horde gold and government bonds, sending prices up.

I expect the same thing in our coming depression with this one twist: The massive government of today will undoubtedly intervene by trying to prop up the economy by inflating it— either directly by having the Fed monetize U.S. government debt or indirectly by letting the dollar fall. Until the crisis gets full-blown, I expect gold (after inflation is factored out) to underperform other commodity assets like grains.

As for U.S. government bonds, one has to remember that the real U.S. debt is not the official $5 trillion or so, but $20–$25 trillion in unfunded pensions (like the Social Security for baby boomers), loan guarantees (everything from Fannie Mae to protecting the solvency of the top 200 banks), plus every sort of subsidy like crop and flood insurance. The bond market is going to take a triple hit of rising inflation, a private credit crunch, plus the likelihood (when the deficit rises to $600 billion and interest payments take all the revenue generated by the income tax) of some sort of government game with interest payments.

---

1 "Prices," Macmillan, 1933

The 16-2/3 Year Production Cycle

The next long-term cycle that I think investors should watch is the 16-$\frac{2}{3}$ year production cycle. This cycle has repeated 49 times since 1289, when it affected wrought-iron prices. I believe it is the basic production cycle of the world economy. During the twentieth century, this cycle has had the pattern shown in Table 14-2:

Table 14-2
The 16-2/3Year Production Cycle

Cycle Low	First High (30 percent)	Midpoint Low	Second Higher High (70 percent)
1982.60	1987.60	1990.93	1994.26
1965.93	1970.88	1974.33	1977.60
1949.28	1954.22	1957.61	1960.93
1932.60	1937.60	1940.93	1944.28
1915.89	1920.89	1924.21	1927.60
1899.22	1902.55	1907.55	1912.55

I have used this cycle, along with the major sunspot and lunar cycles (more on the lunar cycles in the grain section that ends this chapter), to get a pretty good approximation of the stock market over the last 150 years. It's just another indication that the next few years are not going to be times of economic prosperity or a booming stock market.

The Kitchin Cycle

A 41-month, approximately 3-1/2 year cycle was discovered by the economist Kitchin near the turn of the century. According to Dewey, a group of investors used it very successfully in the stock market around World War I. The 41-month cycle can be traced back to the Civil War and beyond. However, there were two problems with using it.

First, to quote Dewey: "In 1946 something strange happened to our cycle. Where stocks used to bottom they now topped and vice versa. Almost as if some giant hand had reached down and pushed it, the cycle stumbled and by the time it had regained its equilibrium it was marching completely out of step... no one can positively explain what happened in 1946."

Actually the explanation is relatively simple. Thanks to 91 percent top tax rates and the huge government debt overhanging the economy, the United States became the first debt-driven economy. Before, stock and bond yields rose together as good business times increased the demand for credit. Now, low interest rates are the lifeblood of business expansion. As interest rates climb, high-income investors have to shut off their investing.

The tax reform of 1986 lowered and equalized tax rates. With no capital gain differential, there was less incentive to finance investment through borrowing. As a result, stocks rose at the same time credit demand rose. That's why interest rates and stock prices peaked together for the first time since World War II in 1987.

I prefer this explanation to that catch-all phrase of frustrated cycle observers: phase shift ("In 1946, the 41-month stock cycle had a phase shift"). In reality, the same phenomenon was occurring—a regular up-and-down increase in credit demand. Government policy had changed the rules so that increased credit demand was bad for business, not a sign of a healthy economy.

The second problem is that this cycle is not a regular 41 months, but seems to slip around up and down about a month. I think the Kitchin cycle is a harmonic of several larger cycles, such as the 100- and 144-year cycles, which are very close, but not quite the same. However, for our purposes, Table 14-3 has successfully predicted bond tops and bottoms plus stock tops since the phase shift after World War II.

Table 14-3
The Post-World-War-II 3.45-Year Kitchin Cycle
(Inflation Adjusted)

Bond Yield High	Bond Yield Low	Stock High
1994.75	1997.05	
1991.30	1993.6	1994
1987.85	1990.15	1990.55
1984.40	1986.70	1987.10
1980.95	1983.25	1983.65
1977.50	1979.80	1980.20
1974.05	1976.35	1976.75
1970.60	1972.90	1973.3
1967.15	1969.45	1969.85
1963.70	1966	1966.4
1960.25	1962.55	1962.95
1956.80	1959.10	1959.50
1953.35	1955.64	1956.05
1949.70	1952.20	1952.60

I used this 3.45-year cycle in 1988 to conclude that the stock market was headed upward until at least 1990.

The 3.45-cycle peak in bond yields is due the end of September or early October, but I suspect election-year politics might delay any final Federal Reserve action on short-term interest rates until after October. Until investors are sure the Fed finally has bitten the bullet on short-term interest rates, they will hesitate to buy.

However, any rally next year in bonds will be short-lived. I don't believe bonds will be a good investment until mid-1996 when the long-term cycle bottom in the depression is due and the end of the Clinton administration will be in sight.

Shorter-Term Cycles in Stocks and Bonds

Virtually everything that has been written about cycles specifically for a futures perspective has concentrated on cycles with a period of less than three months. This fits in with the "tiny-into-a-trillion, daytrade-our-way-to-millions-attitude" that infects many futures traders. It's not that short-term cycles don't have some validity, but there are so many of them operating at once, a novice trader or someone not familiar with all the various cycles can make horrendous mistakes.

One mistake is to assume that real-world cycles are like those on oscilloscopes: perfect sine waves up and down. Another is to assume the pattern will continue forever. Just like the 41-month stock cycle phase shift, that up-and-down pattern you are seeing has an underlying cause—and if you don't understand it, you may mishandle the cycle in your analysis.

I have four suggestions for those of you who must know about shorter-term signals. The first is to borrow every book you can on cycles in futures. You can also buy them, but from what I've seen, not many are very good.

The second is to join the Foundation for the Study of Cycles (2600 Michelson Dr., Suite 1570, Irvine, CA 92715). Their magazine, *Cycles*, has excellent articles, and they do excellent work on short-term cycles, which they release to their members. This is the conclusion of one mid-1989 work on the stock market: "Both the short-term cycles and the 24.08-month cycle are now pointing to a top in September/early October 1989." To reach this conclusion, they used a synthesis of 10 major cycles ranging in length from 11.2 market days to two years. Generating this type of cycle firepower is beyond the range of most futures investors.

My third suggestion is to use a Gann technique. It is possible to count forward in calendar days from previous lows and highs and give reasonable projections of the next tops and bottoms based on standard ratios like Fibonacci numbers. You can use software like Nature's Pulse (Kasanjian Research, P.O. Box 4608, Blue Jay, CA 92317; 1-909-337-0816) to do this work.

My final suggestion is to look up the solar and lunar eclipses and other phases of the moon (such as perigee and apogee) in the *Astronomical Almanac*, published by the Superintendent of Documents (U.S. Government Printing Office, Washington, DC 20402) and available in most libraries. You can also buy the *American Ephemeris* for $9.95 from A.C.S. Publishing, P.O.

Box 34487, San Diego, CA 92613-4487; 1-800-888-9983.

Any astronomical extreme is important in determining a potential top or bottom in the various markets—parallels to the celestial equator and ecliptic among the suns and planets, combinations like solstices and perigees of the moon, etc. Frankly, the complexities of astronomy are beyond me, and I suspect they are beyond the average investor. But I do think a knowledge of what is going on with the moon is worth the extra effort.

In 1993, Burton Pugh proposed that the price of wheat moved higher on the full moon and lower on the new moon. Moon trading has also been advocated by Larry Williams and others. Our word *lunacy* comes from *luna*, Latin for moon. Of all the celestial bodies, the moon seems to have the most powerful influence on human behavior. Since our bodies are 90 percent water, the phases of human behavior seem to move up and down with the moon, just like the tides. Dewey cites a study that 17 percent more babies were born during the waxing periods of the moon than during the waning periods. In some years, that figure was 25 percent!

The sun is 26 million times larger than the moon but it is 359 times farther away from earth. Therefore, the moon exerts two-and-a-half times the gravitational force on us than the sun. The moon's orbit is an ellipse that moves it closer or further away from the earth. All planets move in ellipses, so the sun's gravitational power does fluctuate with its distance to earth, but not every 28 days as with the moon apogee/perigee cycle.

Cycles should be checked for currency and inflation adjustments. This is just as important in my opinion as detrending, averaging to take out randomness, and other standard techniques to find cycles.

3.72- and 7.43-Year Cycles in Currencies and Grains

Every 22.29 years, sunspots complete a cycle of two waves. Sunspots travel in magnetized pairs. In one wave, positively charged spots lead in the sun's northern hemisphere, while negative spots lead in the sun's southern hemisphere. In the next wave, this pattern is reversed.

The orbit of the moon is not exactly the same plane as the orbit of the earth around the sun. It is inclined five degrees. When the moon crosses the plane of the earth (the ecliptic), this is a called a node. The planes become the same (relative to the positions of the stars) every 18.6 years (to be exact, every 6,585.36 days. In other words, every 18.61 years the node makes a complete revolution around the zodiac).

Both cycles topped in the summer of 1973, a peak for grains in purchasing power that hasn't been equaled since. The following one-third subcycle of the 22.29 sunspot cycle and the one-fifth cycle of the 18.6-year lunar cycle correlate almost exactly to grain tops:

1. 7.43-year cycle grain tops: 1973.6, 1981.04, 1988.46, and now 1995.89?

2. .372-year cycle grain tops: 1973.6, 1977.32, 1981.04, 1984.76, 1988.48, 1992.20 (remember the time of the El Niño banner?), and now 1995.92?

The conjunction of these two cycles creates the biggest bull markets in grains. The target date of 1995.98 also agrees with our Analogous Year analysis that grains are due for a price increase over the next one to two years.

These cycles also seem to be connected to the dollar. As inflation fears peak with the price of grains (7.43-year cycle peak), dollar holders look for more stable currencies or to precious metals:

* 1958.64: Despite a U.S. recession, gold begins to flow out of the U.S. This was the start of the chronic balance-of-payments crisis we are still suffering. The weak Canadian dollar and British pound were strong during this period, while hard currencies like the Swiss franc and the deutsche mark began to inch up against the dollar from their post-World-War-II fixed price.

* 1966.17: The U.S. begins to liquidate silver in a desperate attempt to control inflation and prevent the break up of

Bretton Woods. It was also the last year of a stable British pound.

* 1973.6: The U.S. dollar was nearing the end of a sickening plunge, saved later on in the year by rising oil prices.

* 1981.03: Inflation peaks, and the U.S. dollar is beginning to rise from historic lows. Peak of short-term interest rates.

* 1988.46: Dollar doom at its height. There was an almost universal consensus that the U.S. dollar would renew its recent slide against most foreign currencies.

Conversely, the middle of the 7.43-year cycle (which corresponds to the tops of the 3.72-year grain cycle) has seen a fairly strong dollar within the context of a long-term fall of the dollar since the mid-1960s:

* 1962.45: British pound under pressure, along with Canadian dollar.

* 1969.45: Despite Vietnam inflation, the U.S. dollar sees its last days of relative stability for a very long time. French franc at a low against the dollar.

* 1977.31: The peak of the Carter years, before the long slide down.

* 1984.74: The beginning of the surge that would carry the dollar to post-war highs in the blow-off top created by the international euphoria that followed Reagan's reelection. (Just track what happens to the dollar when a U.S. president proposes a tax cut versus tax increase, or when a president acts tough or spends more on defense vs. the opposite.)

* 1992.17: A peak during the awful Bush years. Those who knew Bush best (foreigners) liked him even less than American voters did in 1992. The dollar made a record low in late August/early September 1992 when foreigners thought that Bush might have a chance to be reelected (Bush's poll numbers after the Republican

convention were almost even with Clinton's).

Mild inflation (the middle of the 7.43-year cycle) helps re-source-producers like the United States. Heavy inflation creates panic and a flight out of the dollar. Along with a cycle top in grains, I expect a major low in the dollar come late 1995 or early 1996.

Large currency fluctuations began in 1958, but the same 7.43-year pattern in the dollar can be traced back through the nineteenth century using inflation and what the price of gold bought in the way of a basket of commodities. For example, the dollar reached a peak against major currencies like the pound near the time the 7.43-year cycle predicted would be a period of strength: 1932.72.

These last two cycles are a perfect example of the synergy or resonation you must use to make long-term cycle predictions. By themselves, the 3.72-year and 7.43-year cycles in grains are inter-esting, but they become even more validated when you realize currency fluctuations are moving along the same lines.

Virtually every long-term cycle agrees with our other indi-cators (like Analagous Year) that 1994 is a time to sell stocks and bonds and buy commodities, especially grains. If you know the market bias of the next few years—securities (especially stocks) down, commodities (especially grains) up—you have an im-mense advantage over the average investor. Even a strict tech-nician must adjust his chart patterns and indicators to the shift from a bull to a bear market and vice versa. If I am close to being right in the above predictions, this will be worth many times the price of this book even if you never use any specific technique in your trading.

Chapter Fifteen

The Media: The Best Trading Indicator

Back when I worked for what I later found out was a phony econometric firm, I had a conversation with one of its principals, whom I'll call "Stan." Stan used to trade on the floor of the Comex in the silver pit. He told me two things I'll never forget.

Before the opening or when trading was dull, he used to chit-chat with all the filling brokers who executed trades for the major stock houses and discount firms. His patter would go something like this: "Hi, Ira. How's the wife and kids? Did you have a good weekend? How many to sell at 95?" The last sentence was a request for the number of December silver contract sell-stop orders at 6.95 Ira had in his deck. Of course this is supposed to be illegal and maybe floor traders now aren't as blatant as Stan used to be. But floor traders have other ways of finding out where the stops are. They've got the same indicators and charts. All the major newsletters and hotlines are upstairs at the exchange library. They can send their clerks to read every one of them and tell them where the stops are.

Stan told me one other thing that started me down the path of writing this chapter. Whenever I was too long silver and needed to get out, I'd just call up the commodity reporter at *The*

Wall Street Journal and give him every reason for being long silver. The reporter would write the story, the story would appear in *The Journal,* the orders would flow into the pits from thousands of traders all over the country, and Stan and his buddies would get out of their long silver positions and go short.

I have said it before and it bears repeating: reporters get paid $50,000 a year to generate stories. If one comes gift-wrapped and ready to print from a reputable source like Stan the Floor Trader, why shouldn't that reporter save some time and print it as is?

After all, there is always a long for every short in the futures market. At any given moment, there's always a case for the bulls and a case for the bears. Whatever side the newspaper prints is an editorial judgment. If someone else is willing to take the risk of putting his name on a market call, so much the better. Anybody who's angry can call up Stan the Floor Trader and complain to him. Don't blame *The Wall Street Journal* for printing someone else's opinion!

When I was a futures broker, I saw other brokers use a *Wall Street Journal* article to sell a trade dozens of times (for stocks and bonds as well as futures). Even when the futures trade lost (the normal result), there was less anger and resentment among the clients. Didn't we see it in the great *Wall Street Journal*? "At least I went down with the best information available," the client would rationalize.

I often tell the story of Stan the Floor Trader at seminars. Then I usually ask, "Do you think it is routine for market insiders to feed the media stories?" Only a few hands go up in the room—usually the ones from Europe. For some reason Europeans have no trouble with the concept of a manipulated media, but Americans are determined to believe that everything they read is on the up-and-up.

After I wrote an article about media trading for *Technical Analysis of Stocks and Commodities* magazine, people called from around the world, begging me to give them more information.

I always felt bad when I had to tell foreigners I'd only done research on American business media. The ones that wanted help the most were the ones I could help the least.

Besides a reluctance to disbelieve what they read, American futures traders also don't like a method you can't put in a computer. Yes, I've done word studies using headlines in the business press. There is a difference in market action between use of the word *plunge* in the headline rather than *fall*. And I do share these results with clients. But learning how to read the media is an art. It's very hard, if not impossible, to computerize everything. For example, the position of the story is very important. You can ask the computer to find the word *plunge* on the C-1 page of *The Wall Street Journal*. But how do you tell it to look for *plunge* in the headline that leads the top right-hand column? Is there a chart? Is *plunge* in smaller type in a secondary sentence?

I really feel that the greatest reason why media trading is not a standard technique is the fact that it cannot be computerized or easily predigested. Of course, a lot of firms don't want to bite the hand that feeds them. Why antagonize the paper that runs your ads by telling everyone how lousy their advice is? But it really is amazing how little discussion of media trading there is when you consider how many big names like Richard Band, Ned Davis, Paul Macrae Montgomery, etc., have advocated using the business press as a contrary opinion indicator.

Even Gann talked about the effects of the media in *Truth of the Stock Tape* (Pomeroy, Washington: Lambert-Gann, 1976). And *Reminiscences of a Stock Operator* has a whole section on how the nameless operator used the effects of a news article to unload his massive long position in cotton over the space of a few minutes.

I've even seen one of Richard Dennis' famous turtles discuss media trading in his newsletter! Dennis is a technical trading legend who decided to teach a select group (the turtles) some of his methods. If one of Dennis' disciples can take his eyes off the Sacred Six long enough to say, "I think newspaper headlines are a great thing to fade," perhaps you should fade them, too!

The Basics of Media Trading

Since media trading has to be somewhat of an art rather than an exact science, there are many things about it that can never be precisely pinned down. There are at least three basic problems that face every media trader no matter how long he has studied the subject and used media trading techniques in making his trading decisions.

1. Determining what's important: is it news or is it emotional bias?

2. Judging the signal's intensity.

3. Is the signal long, intermediate, or short term?

I will spend the rest of the chapter discussing these issues. But before I get to those three basic problems, there is one media trading problem that isn't really a problem at all.

A Problem That Isn't a Problem When Reading the Media

The answer to the question, "How long does the effect of an article or TV program last on the markets?" is simply our old Rule of Three working with the 3/21-Day Memory Law.

Just like any market event, a media story—whether print or electronic—has the most impact during the first three hours after someone has seen it. Over the next three days, 80 percent of the contents of that story will slip from the memory. After three weeks, only 3 percent of that article will be remembered. It will then become part of the permanent memory. This memory will not normally be triggered unless a similar event occurs: "I see beans were up the limit on a drought scare. Didn't the Journal run a drought story a month ago on beans?"

In dealing with a print article, the maximum impact of that article will be on the morning it comes out. Most people read their paper every morning. Just like the opening routines of the market, if an article fails (a bullish story does not lead to a market reversal down by the end of the day, or vice versa for a bearish story), we can anticipate another three days of market action in the direction (bullish or bearish) of the article. If, after three days, there is another failure (no market reversal in the direction against the thrust of the article), then we can expect three weeks of market action in the direction of that story leading to a major top or bottom.

Few people videotape or take notes of their favorite business TV show. The vast majority of those who watch TV business shows don't do either. In my opinion, the impact of all TV business shows, even celebrated ones like "Wall Street Week," does not extend much beyond three days.

You should keep a diary of the business articles you read and the business TV shows you see. It will increase your faith in media trading as you see how the media was always screamingly bullish at major tops and obviously bearish at major bottoms. So by all means, keep anything you've written down for future reference. But as far as market decisions are concerned, you don't need to refer to any media comment more than four weeks old.

The Logistics of Media Trading

One of the problems of trading is the sheer logistics of it: 90 percent of your most important trading decisions are made before 10:00 A.M. It can be overwhelming. No wonder so many go to a black-box system that tells them exactly what to do 15 minutes after the previous close.

But if you are going to use something besides a pure mechanical approach in your trading, the media system actually saves time. You don't need to refer to anything but the last three to four weeks of media commentary. The rest can go into storage for leisurely study. The headlines of the media tell you which market you should look at to trade. You don't have to calculate expected range, etc., for every market; you need to figure only the ones the media says you should consider.

In fact, media trading is one of the few trading approaches I know where you don't have to have a computer and fancy software (although having a computer does cut down the drudgery time). A subscription to *The Wall Street Journal* provides you with virtually every market quote, including most cash markets. Add in the other national dailies and your own regional paper, a trip to the library for all the weekly business periodicals, and you are set.

Because that's far cheaper than $750 a month for the quotes, software, and seminars routine of black-box trading, you have a chance to survive by not violating the Mathematics of Investing. Because it's easier to trade longer term with the media (you can ignore the smaller movements until the media blares at you, "This is a top," or "This is a bottom"), you don't have to be a quote-machine slave. You can work another job until you know that you are good enough to trade full time.

Media trading teaches you discipline and patience. You learn to wait until all the conditions are right. Unless the media "speaks," you stay in your winning positions even though your emotions are screaming, "Take profits! Take profits!" You avoid getting prematurely into positions and, most importantly, you learn how to reverse yourself completely when conditions warrant it.

Media trading is the answer to a small trader's prayer. He needs something that is cheap to operate and will force him to be careful when entering positions and patient with his winners. He also needs something that doesn't bore him into overtrading. Reading the media every day is like an adventure—you don't know what to expect but you know you will never be bored. Even if there is no signal trading-wise, the circus of human existence (politics, sports, etc.) is there on the printed page to entertain you, even if there is nothing to do in the markets.

Determining What's Important: Is It News or Is It Emotional Bias?

The first problem in any media trading system is to determine what is actually important for your trading, what is routine and unimportant, and what should make you stand up and take notice.

The first step is to determine what you can afford to read. Ideally, you should get four papers each business day before the trading day (you can go to the library for the weekend editions): *The Wall Street Journal*, the *New York Times*, *U.S.A. Today*, and your biggest local regional paper.

I'm fortunate that my local paper, the *Chicago Tribune*, is the most prominent regional paper for trading futures—it reaches more Midwestern farmers than any other paper and has special coverage of the local futures markets. If grain trading is your specialty, you should make every effort to get the *Tribune*. Back in rain-soaked July 1993—the very day the grain market topped—*The Wall Street Journal* ran a story on page A-1, top right-hand column, on the destruction of the soybean crop due to excess rain. That gave a powerful media sell signal. But the icing on the cake, the story that really steeled the trading backbone to go short, was a simultaneous front-page story in the *Tribune* about the same topic.

But even if your biggest local regional paper is not the *Tribune* but the *Detroit Free Press*, the *St. Louis Post-Dispatch*, the *Miami Herald*, the *Atlanta Constitution*, etc., it is still a valuable trading tool, especially for stock and bond trading. If some market makes the headlines of your local paper, it is a very powerful media signal.

If you get these four daily papers now, so much the better. But if you don't, then you must treat any additional subscription as a business decision. You must use Dull-but-Successful Trading Rule #1 (see p. 27) If you have a $5,000 account and the interest you generate on the account is 4 percent a year, or $200, you really don't have much room to maneuver. If your account size leaves you a little short, then here is the order in which I would add additional papers:

1. *The Wall Street Journal*: It's the premier business paper in the country and the only readily available source for all market quotes, including the cash markets.

2. The next paper you get depends on whether you have another reason to trade besides speculation, i.e., whether

you are a bona fide hedger. If you are a grain farmer, you should get the *Chicago Tribune* if it is readily available in your area. If you are a jeweler or a fuel-oil distributor or some other dealer in a future that is traded in New York, you should get the *New York Times*.

3. If you are not a bona fide hedger, the order I suggest for adding new papers after *The Journal* is the *New York Times*, *U.S.A. Today*, then your local major regional paper and *Investor's Business Daily*.

I live in an area that has many libraries. Even if one library is missing a copy of a weekend edition of a paper or a weekly periodical, I can always go to another library that is close by. But if you live in an area with inadequate libraries, you may have to, as your account size grows, pay to get these weekly periodicals in this order of priority:

1. *Barron's*

2. *Forbes*

3. *U.S. News & World Report*

4. *The Economist* (from the U.K.)

5. *Business Week*

6. *Fortune*

7. *Futures*

8. *Time*

9. *Newsweek*

10. Weekend editions of your regional paper and the *New York Times*.

If you look at all the assets you own, you may find out you are really trading a lot more in the future market than you think; your trading position includes personal assets like gold and stocks, a variable-rate mortgage, etc. Then you can justify spending more on your futures trading account than Dull-but-Successful Trading Rule #1 would justify. You can count part of the $6,000 or so you are making in dividends with $200,000 in stocks toward what you can spend on quotes, newspapers, etc., in your futures account.

Nearly everyone has a TV and can watch such free programs as the "Nightly Business Report," network news, and "Wall Street Week." TV programs are often your best indicator of a near-term top or bottom because TV's impact is so limited in terms of time. Most people get cable. If you don't have cable, you should consider getting it for the quotes and comments on CNBC's daytime financial program. CNBC's weekend roundtable program of various financial pundits is also a great way to find out the market consensus, a consensus that is almost always wrong.

There are two major disadvantages of media trading. One is the cost of buying all these periodicals if you don't have an adequate library. And you can't get periodicals, let alone daily papers, if you live on a mountaintop somewhere.

All of life is choices. If you want to daytrade, you really should move to Chicago or New York and learn how to do it in the proper venue—the exchange floor. If you want to live in the wilderness, far from any sizable town, you are going to have to rely on the price quotes and commentary that comes over your satellite dish. If you want the added dimension of media trading, you can't just live anywhere.

Remember the *Tribune* and *The Wall Street Journal* article that occurred at the very top of the 1993 bean market? If you were a farmer with 100,000 bushels of beans (20 contracts) to sell, it would have been a very expensive proposition if you got these papers only in the mail. Those stories occurred on Friday, July 23, 1993. The opening on the August beans was 7.35 a bushel that day. The following Monday's opening was 7.17. The next day's opening was 7.095—the highest opening for months to come. Depending on what time you got the papers in the mail, you could have been up to 25 cents a bushel behind the original media trading signal. A $25,000 difference ain't hay!

A farmer with 100,000 bushels of soybeans growing in the

field or stored in his elevator has $700,000 (at 7.00 a bushel for cash soybeans) tied up in inventory. If he sold his growing or stored crop in the cash-forward market to the local grain elevator, he should be able to pay his bills and still have plenty of money to go long or short the equivalent amount of beans on the futures market, 20 contracts. The margin on 20 contracts of bean futures would be only around $30,000. Wouldn't it have been better for that farmer to lose the whole $30,000 than to watch his 100,000 bushels of beans drop $100,000 as the price fell from 7.00 to 6.00 on the cash market, as it did later in 1993?

After getting the number of periodicals appropriate to your circumstances, the next step is to learn how to read them. Some things are obvious. You can read the sports and entertainment sections later. If you are reading four papers in the morning, you really only have about 10 minutes for each one before you run into the all-important openings and the first trading decisions of the day.

It would be nice to read every pertinent article all the way through, but that's not necessary. A lot of people who read *The Wall Street Journal*, the *New York Times*, etc., are in the same boat you are. They are only going to be able to skim the headlines and the major stories of the day. It's their quick, emotional response to the news that puts in the tops and bottoms of markets. All you are really looking for is the headlines of stories and the charts and pictures that accompany them. As the trite-but-true cliche has it, "A picture is worth a thousand words." The body of the story may have all the boring details that contradict the headline and the charts at the front of the story, but few people have the time or the energy to read everything carefully.

There are two styles of newspaper. *The Wall Street Journal* under its "What's News" column summarizes most of that paper's major stories. The *New York Times* has the traditional layout where any story summaries are on the second page or the front of each section, like the business section. This leads us to the first of my media trading rules:

1. *Every important investment turning point gets put on the front page or the front cover.*

Every important move in the futures market will end up in the front page of some national newspaper or the front cover of a major business magazine. Even relatively minor markets like coffee can get to the front page, as it did recently in the July 11, 1994, *U.S.A. Today*, two days before coffee topped (at least so far in 1994).

2.   *In all markets, every important top (and most bottoms) gets prominent mention by more than one national media source.*

I keep a weekly diary of headlines from the various media sources segregated into one page each for the trillion-dollar markets: currencies, interest rates, stocks, metals, crude complex, and agricultural markets. My sheets for the stock market for the weeks March 28–April 1, 1994, and April 2–8, 1994, look like a war zone. I can hardly fit all the references on a single page. It doesn't take a genius to see the message the media were sending out: "Hey, dummy, your stocks are down 10 percent. Don't you think you'd better do something to protect yourself (like sell out)?" If you have the patience and wait for these obvious signs (front-page headlines, a market featured by every news source in a prominent way), you will be well rewarded.

You can, if you wish, weight each story by the size and prestige of the publication, where in the publication it is, etc., to come up with a media index that will give you the intensity of each story. This will also help the more experienced media trader sharpen his or her skills. But the more I see of the media, the more I think this isn't necessary, especially for the novice trader. Just like Pavlov's dogs, the media ring the bell loud and clear at tops and bottoms. Your biggest problem is not to be swept up in the emotion and ignore the signal.

For example, I am not thrilled with long-term prospects of the stock market. But the media signal of the last week in March and the first week of April was so strong you had to go with it. It was an intermediate bottom in the stock market that a futures trader had to respect, even if the long-term, multiyear trend had turned down.

3.   *A media signal is inversely proportional to the extravagance*

of the language used to describe a market event.

Some exaggerated media language is easy to see—like "Bonds Bask in Best of All Worlds" (in the current yield section of the January 31, 1994, edition of *Barron's*), or "Like Old Times— An Era of Low Inflation Changes the Calculus for Buyers and Sellers," a page A-1 headline of the January 14, 1994, *Wall Street Journal*. But extravagant language goes on all the time in the media. To check for it, I like to use one paper as a measuring stick.

Many people ask me if there are any common media outlets you don't fade—investment publications whose headlines aren't always or usually bad trading advice. My reply is, "If your library has it displayed in your reading room, you can usually 'fade' what it says." If there are any exceptions to this rule, the *Economist* magazine of England and *Investor's Business Daily* are those exceptions.

I discuss the *Economist* later in this chapter, but *Investor's Business Daily* is a very good illustration of Rule #3 above. This paper's headlines are usually very precise and accurate, and typically there is an attempt to get both sides (bull and bear) of any market—if not in the headlines of one day, at least with a series of articles over time. Most of the regular features make sense—the futures that rose or fell the most are featured on the futures page, the bond page is a very accurate description of what moved the bond market that day, etc. *Investor's* makes a good contrast with the other national and regional papers. Of course, in the rare times it does feature market predictions, *Investor's* is normally as bad as anyone on the street. But it understands that its main mission is not to patronize its readers with investment pontifications.

4. *The more unexpected a headline, the greater the media signal.*

If *The Wall Street Journal* puts soybeans on the front pages, that's unexpected. If the *New York Times* or *U.S.A. Today* has a banner headline about stocks on its front page, you can expect at least a minor trend change in stocks usually within three days. On the other hand, if a big stock movement doesn't make the front page of *The Wall Street Journal* the next day (as happened the Monday following a near-100-point drop on Friday February 4, 1994), that's significant. Instead, the *Journal* had a soothing C-1 article that read, "Most Expect Stock Market to Rebound." To me, this negated the usual long-term implications of a front-page *New York Times* headline on a Dow plunge (this also was on Saturday, which has a much weaker market impact).

It's pretty rare, but when the media make a howling, obvious error, you can expect a countermove to begin. The headlines of the June 22, 1994, *Wall Street Journal* commodity page read: "Gold Hits Highest Levels in 10 months." Any way you look at it—closest-to-cash gold future or the afternoon London gold fix; closing basis or high of the day—gold prices were not at a 10-month high. They were several dollars below their January 1994 highs. You could blame this on midsummer madness or another sneak attack of Stan the Floor Trader. In any case, this was a top that held for several months.

One of the strongest media signals you can get—because it is so unexpected—is the warning. By warning I don't mean the usual commodity bashing or the attacks on the "barbarous relic," gold. But if a leading medium starts to warn you about the high price of either stocks or bonds, it's a sign that a top is far away. In August 1993, *The Wall Street Journal* went on a campaign to convince everyone that the bond market was a lousy place to be. On August 10, 1993, an A-1 column 6 headline (the strongest they could run) screamed "Portfolio Surprise: Many Americans Run Hidden Financial Risk from Derivatives." Then, on August 17, another A-1 right-hand column: "Managing Risk: Corporate Treasurers Adopt Hedging Plans With Some Wariness." And finally, an August 30 A-1 right-hand headline: "Inverse Relationship: Despite Risks, Many Investors Keep Buying Bond Funds." The lead of the third paragraph read, "Those risks are huge; today, in fact, bonds may be riskier than stocks." Bonds riskier than stocks! I can't remember a similar statement being made by any leading business publication!

In my opinion, it was no accident this campaign started on August 10, just about three weeks before its peak on August 30.

Nor is it a coincidence that bond prices went higher for the next three weeks and ultimately peaked six weeks later in October. What are tops made of? Premature bears and angry baby bulls! Nothing was better calculated to send a market higher than the August campaign of warnings. Low-capitalized shorts were encouraged to enter only to be squeezed out. Cautious bulls that refrained from buying in August due to the warnings angrily bought twice as much in September and October, furious that they had missed a great move and determined not to miss another one.

I have a theory of August/early September versus late September/early October. The brain of the average investor reaches its most susceptible state in late August/early September. If he isn't on an actual vacation, his reactions have been dulled by lying around in the sun all summer. He is easy prey to suggestions, especially those from the media. Then, like a startled sleepwalker, he snaps awake around the fall equinox. His first reaction is to make up for the lethargy of summer with a frenzied burst of action. Since the natural tendency of the investor is to buy, that's what he does.

Gann supposedly claimed that capital and commodity markets tended to top on or around September 22 more often than any day of the year (a thing to keep in mind as we watch the 1994 stock market making a double-top). I don't know whether or not Gann actually said this, but there is significant evidence that this is true. On or about September 22, all of the following occurred:

* All-time highs in corn (1974), cotton (1973), and gold and silver stocks (many oil stocks made a peak at the same time in 1980).
* Peak of Dow-Jones utility index in 1929.
* Secondary peak of gold in 1980, stocks in 1987.
* Major top in soybeans, 1983.
* Date of major devaluation of the pound (1931 and 1992) and major devaluation of the dollar (Plaza Accord of 1985).

* Peak in the bond market for many years (1993).

5. *Even when the media tell you the truth about a market, it's never at the best time to take action.*

When *The Journal* issued its August 1993 warnings about the bond market, it was absolutely correct in pointing the finger at the derivative market as the primary source of danger in any market turnaround. But this correct warning was buried under the big rise in bonds during September and October, never to be remembered again.

On May 27, 1994, *The Wall Street Journal* commodity page headline blared, "Cattle Prices Jump Daily Limit, Bouncing Back from a Sharp Drop that May Have Hit Bottom." The next trading day, the following Tuesday, May 31, cattle hit a top that held for the next month and a half. But it was true that cattle prices were only a few weeks away from what looks now like a multiyear bottom.

On March 28, 1994, the Foreign Exchange section of *The Wall Street Journal* had a headline of "Antagonism Toward Dollar May Be Due to Fundamentals, Not Fleeting Factors." I think that was and is still true, but three days after this report, the U.S. dollar index began a 2.5-basis-point move upward.

The June 1993 *Futures* magazine printed this very good piece of long-term advice: "Commodity Indexes Hint Return of Inflation." Two of the subheadlines were, "Commodity prices have hit rock bottom," and "My assumption is the downtrend in commodity prices that began in 1980 ended in February 1993." In my opinion, both these statements were true, but it took about three weeks after *Futures* hit the newsstands and the mailboxes before the CRB finally bottomed out for the month and renewed its climb upward.

6. *What the media expect almost never happens.*

Now we have seen from the last three examples that occasionally the media bumble into making a good long-term call. But by far the usual process is just awful market predictions. For example, the February 18, 1994, *Wall Street Journal* commodity page headline was, "Grain Traders Are Anticipating a Spring Rally"—a rally that was two months away and which in any case never exceeded the February 1994 highs in corn.

One more example of failed media expectations appeared on April 1, 1994, with *The Wall Street Journal* commodity headline, "Corn Prices Likely to Rise in Wake of Report That Farmers Plan to Plant Less Than Expected"—well, that was a real April Fooler!

On January 13, 1994, *The Wall Street Journal* commodity page headline read, "Grain Prices Are Expected to Shoot Up as USDA Releases Even Bleaker Estimate." This headline came with a corn chart. Of all the grains they could have picked, they ran the chart of the grain that was going to be the weakest of the whole year. Coincidence? Well, you can believe what you want but, as I said before, floor traders pay for their million-dollar exchange seats with coincidences.

I could have chosen many, many other examples from many, many other publications, but I am picking on *The Wall Street Journal* commodity page for a reason. In October 1989 my article "The Best Trading Indicator—The Media" came out in *Technical Analysis of Stocks and Commodities* magazine. About a year later, full-page ads began to run advertising a daytrade system with wonderful profits, low drawdowns, high accuracy, and the simplicity of needing only a newspaper (no charts, no computers and software). There are a zillion sure-thing systems advertised in every issue of every futures-oriented magazine, but this one caught my eye because it used a quote from my article: "If I had only five minutes a day to read one publication, it would be the commodity page of *The Wall Street Journal*." Intrigued and somewhat annoyed, I politely wrote and asked if I could see the system since my quote was being used in a way that implied my endorsement.

I never got a response, but I finally did get a photocopy from a friend. Mass copying is the fate of all sure-thing systems. I felt justified in getting a photocopy since my quote had probably sold quite a few systems. Here's what you got for $279:

Look at the commodity headline from *The Wall Street Journal*. If it was "Gold Rallies Three Dollars on Russian Fears," you sold gold. If it was "Cattle Plunges," you bought cattle on the opening. To offset the trade, you simply closed out your position on the close.

This is dangerously simplistic and definitely not worth $279 (In my humble opinion, you are going to get a lot more from this chapter). But the amazing thing was, if you took the worst opening prices (highest opening prices if buying, vice versa for selling) and threw in a $30 commission, the blasted thing about broke even.

7. *The indicator the media attack as inaccurate is the indicator you should watch. What the media say you should watch, you can ignore.*

During 1994, there has been a continuous chatter from the media how the CPI overstates inflation and the CRB is a "fickle" gauge of inflation" (in the words of a C-1 *New York Times* article that appeared May 25, 1994). The CPI, like every government statistic, is flawed. Alan Greenspan admitted recently that he is frustrated with the increasingly inaccurate statistics put out by the government. Many blame this on budget cuts inspired by Ronald Reagan.

This free marketer thinks it's the natural consequence of an increasingly complex modern economy being measured by horse-and-buggy economists in the Labor Department. Be that as it may, it's the best indicator we've got, and it does move the markets. I never saw anybody complain that the CPI overstated the *downward* move of inflation during the bond rallies of the 1980s!

8. *If there is a "but" in the headline, the market trend continues.*

There is one media maxim you can easily check out with a computer hook-up to media headline data. If you see something like, "Bonds Advance, but...," bonds are going to continue to advance. If the media excuses away a market action with some contradictory evidence, it's a strong sign that the market will continue in the same direction. "Stocks climb the wall of worry," is the old market adage. You could also say, "Stocks trip down the staircase of bullish excuses."

The Intensity of the Signal

If what to look at is the first basic problem of media trading, then the second major problem is how to judge the intensity of each media signal. Let's use *The Wall Street Journal* to illustrate intensity in an individual print source.

The following quotes are from Jerry Rosenberg's book *Inside the Wall Street Journal:* (New York: Macmillan, 1982).

> Without question the most widely read portion of *The Journal* is the double-column space on its front page titled "What's News." The feature had probably led to more paper sales than any other.... "What's News" takes up two of the six columns on the front page.... [The subheadings] "World Wide" and "Business and Finance" have proved to be a boon to busy executives. A quick perusal is sufficient to keep them abreast of world events [*that* The Journal *thinks they should know!*—G.N.).
>
> Columns one and six and the back-page feature are called "leaders...." The demand [is for] 506 leaders a year.... At vacation times, in early August and early September, for example, the editors often sweat to get the leader columns filled. Two weeks later [*around the fall equinox!*—G.N.] they may be faced with a horrible glut.
>
> Vermont Royster, who retired from *The Journal* in 1971 [*after being their lead editorial writer*—G.N.]...made some interesting comments apropos of the "leader" concept: "I think the newspaper business is already moving in the direction of interpretive reporting. When we first started our leader-type stories, we were innovators.... [Now] large metropolitan newspapers

have adopted this technique.... One of the tasks of journalism in the future is to devise ways and means of backing off a bit from these immediate day-to-day crises and trying to give them some perspective." [Newspapers have followed the lead of *The Wall Street Journal* by shifting from reporting the maximum amount of facts and letting the reader decide their significance to dressing up their editorial bias as news.—G.N.]

Column six is the weightiest column...generally regarded as the most important feature...by the page one staff.... A story that appears in column four...tends to be lightweight, sometimes given to sheer frivolity.

The fifth column [to those who remember their history, this column is aptly named!—G.N.] of *The Journal's* front page carries the "special reports..."

The format of *The Wall Street Journal* is similar to that of all other major newspapers. The top headlines are the most important—you can almost skip the "What's News" headlines after the first article summary. Anything on the right-hand side has the strongest impact, while those headlines in the middle are the weakest. Weakest of all are the headlines below the fold in the C-1 section—those headlines you have to fold out the newspaper to full length to see at all.

In my weekly diary of headlines of each specific trillion-dollar market, I abbreviate these positions (TR is top right, BL would be below left, etc.) along with its position in the paper (Com. for commodity page, Forex for the foreign exchange page, etc.). Just start doing it—you'll be amazed how the subtlest shades of headline positioning and wording affects the markets. No formula I can give you, even if it existed, could replace the confidence and skill you get by seeing how, day after day, the media give you amazing insight into the strength and direction of the markets.

Originally I thought it would be simple to construct a media index to use as a trading signal. There is something to this concept, which is why I am going to give you some rough ways of doing it in the paragraphs below. But if you use media signals as the only indicator, you are asking for trouble. You have to look at other techniques to gauge the true strength of the media signal. This is the third basic problem of media trading, which I discuss later in this chapter.

But for now, here are two rough systems to track the intensity of the media signals you get.

The Intesity Level Tracking System

The first system is the Intensity Level Tracking System. Begin by calculating the *intensity level* of the story:

Level 3 (the highest intensity): Front-page *The Wall Street Journal* and *New York Times.*

Level 2: C-1 (business) headlines of *The Wall Street Journal* (and its commodity page) and the *New York Times*; the front page or front cover of any other media outlet we have mentioned by name so far; lead story of any TV program mentioned.

Level 1: Regular columns (Foreign Exchange, Credit Markets, etc.) of *The Wall Street Journal* or *New York Times* that are buried in the back of their business sections; a feature article or news report of any TV program or print media outlet mentioned so far.

Next, calculate the *market level* of each individual future featured by the media outlet:

Level 3: Anything that is not Level 1 or 2.

Level 2: Bean complex, corn, wheat complex, cattle, hogs, sugar, silver, copper.

Level 1: Stock index futures, any interest-rate future or currency, crude complex, and gold.

To get the impact of a media feature on any specific future, you multiply the media intensity level by the level of the futures importance. For example, a front-page *Wall Street Journal* story on coffee would have a nine impact, or three times three. The higher the total impact number from all sources, the greater the media effect on the future, and the greater the chance a strong, opposite reaction will start later on the same day (or at the very least, within three days) of the appearance of the article or TV program.

If it is a New-York-based publication talking about a New-York-based future, add one to the impact number. If it is a Chicago-based publication talking about a Chicago primary market, do the same thing. If it is the lead paper for stock commentary (*Barron's* or the *Journal*), add one. If the story on bonds is in the *New York Times*, add one to the impact number. If the story is on a London-dominated future, divide the impact number in half. If the *Economist* of London has featured a future in its finance or business section, subtract or add one to the impact number depending on the story line.

The New York Federal Reserve Bank is the leading Fed bank in the country. The official newspaper of choice for well-timed leaks from the Fed is the *New York Times*. The front cover and front sections of the *Economist* are as reliable as any other publication to fade. But the business and financial sections in the back are usually (but by no means always) a very good predictor of the next three months of price action.

President John F. Kennedy said the *Economist* was the most important publication in the world. I think he was talking mainly about its business and financial sections.

The Media Tracking System

My second system is the Media Tracking System, which uses the percentage values below.

WSJ	N.Y Times	U.S.A Today	Barron's	Bus.Week Fortune Forbes	Time Newsweek U.S.News	Futures	Network News	CNBC	PBS
12	9	7	7	7	7	7	4	4	4
6	5	3	3	3	3	3	1	1	1
2	1								

The first line of numbers is the impact-percentage value to be given for a cover story or front-page headline for any given future (the numbers above are simply examples that you can fine-tune for each future) for the media outlet above. The second line is the impact percentage for a major feature article or TV story after the headlines (for example, a C-1 feature in the Journal or *Times*). The final line is the impact percentage for a regular feature of the *Times* or *Journal* buried in the back, such as Foreign Exchange or Credit Markets. The closer the totals are to 100 percent, the greater the media impact.

The Intensity Level System has the virtue of simplicity, while the Media Tracking System can be fine-tuned with each future and where the story is positioned in the media outlet (top right, below middle, is there a chart or picture?, etc.). Have fun playing with the numbers!

Media watching can get overwhelming with all the periodicals, but it pays off. Even the *New York Times* bestseller list (for books) is a great indicator. If the *Depression of 1990* is topping the list, it's time to load up on stocks and bonds. When *Bankruptcy 1995* finally drops off the bestseller list (as it did in August 1993), a bond top was at the door. The federal government going bankrupt? Not with Clinton the budget-cutter! Not with the biggest bull market in bonds in a generation!

In the book *News and the Market* (Chicago: Regnery, 1974), authors Klein and Prestbo used the following system to weight stories in *The Wall Street Journal*:

> The system we decided upon gave a score of three to the lead, or top story in both "What's News" columns; a score of two to stories that appear above the fold that divides the paper in half horizontally; and a score of one to stories below the fold. All items in the "What's News" columns were graded except the daily statistical summaries of the previous day's market activity and the "Company Notes" items....
>
> *The Wall Street Journal* carries three feature stories on its daily front page.... Features we deemed potentially market affecting...were given a value of three, the same as the lead items in the "What's News" columns. The system we used...was simple: stories that seemed to

be...bullish...were give a plus...bearish stories got a minus...stories that were neutral or indifferent got a zero....

Before we embarked on our grading process, we solicited the advice of stockbrokers, security analysts, fellow business journalists, economists, and other observers.... We described our grading system to them in general and told them to evaluate (six) items solely for their potential impact on stocks....

Of the 146 gradable items in the six issues, our evaluations matched the majority of the stockmarket pros on 114, or 78 percent. Of the 32 items on which we and the pros differed, all but three were either scored as zero by our panelists and either plus or minus by us. (pp. 54–55)

Using this system, they tracked the news in *The Wall Street Journal* and the 1972 stock market. "The News Index (had)...the most intense and good news coming from late October through mid-November, when the DJIA posted its most dramatic gains." (p. 98)

The peak of the good-news campaign of 1972 was about two months before the market top in mid-January 1973. *Bankruptcy 1995* dropped out of the bestseller two months before the 1993 top of bonds. *The Wall Street Journal*'s anti-bond campaign started two months before the 1993 bond top.

Two months before the 1993 bond top, Jim Bianco sent me an August 18, 1993, report entitled, "It Wasn't Like This in the 1970s." In it were dozens of price-war stories in the media over the previous six weeks. I guess the idea of the investment firm was to show how wonderful everything was with inflation. Both Jim and I looked at the report and said, "It's a top (for bonds)."

I could also add that the NASDAQ high was made about two months after the media euphoria ("New Era, Best of All Possible Worlds") of January 1994. I guess this two-month media rule can be considered an offshoot of the three-month segment of the Rule of Three.

Is the Signal Long, Intermediate, or Short Term?

Richard Band, in his wonderful chapter, "I saw it in the *New York Times*" from his book *Contrary Investing for the '90s* (New York: St. Martin, 1989), stated that the hardest problem in judging a media signal is to distinguish primary from intermediate, intermediate from short. We can use the Rule of Three, the intensity of the signal, etc., to give us some idea of where a media signal is taking the market. But, at best, that gives us only the outlook for the next three weeks.

Three weeks is an eternity for most futures traders, but looking ahead for the next three months or even the next three years is necessary to trade effectively. In any case, the Psychological Law of 10/20 Percent says we can't base any more than 20 percent of our trading decisions on the media, no matter how good a signal it is.

So we must fall back on other techniques like Analogous Year, First through the Even, Inflation- and Currency-Adjusted Charts, etc., to get this longer-term perspective. Let me give you examples of some of the real-life problems you run into with media trading.

The August 31, 1987, *U.S. News & World Report* had a cover of a bucking bull and the caption, "The Bull Market—Time to Get Out?" But in August 1987, *U.S. News* was the least influential news weekly of the three major news weeklies (way below *Time* and *Newsweek* in terms of prestige and readership. In its August 10, 1987, issue the far more influential *Barron's* cover had a bull running away from a lot of overweight business types with the caption: "Memo to the Pros: In Case You Haven't Noticed, the Bull Market Is Beating the Pants Off You." *U.S. News & World Report* was virtually alone in its warning on stocks.

Today, *U.S. News & World Report* is probably the leading news weekly, now that *Time* has become more politically correct. Under the leadership of the very-well-connected Morton Zuckerman, *U.S. News* is right on top of the pack: a cover story of the "Best Mutual Funds" in the February 7, 1994, issue and a June 14, 1994, article entitled, "Why Market Bulls Are Headed for Trouble."

I've discussed how the February 4, 1994, Saturday front-page headline of the "Plunging Dow" in the *New York Times* was more than negated by the nonchalant way *The Wall Street Journal* treated a 96-point Dow drop the following Monday. *Investor's Daily* had a small, below-the-fold, front-page article just before this Dow collapse talking about how the market might be overvalued. *Newsweek* in its February 15 issue ran an article "Beware the Baby Bull."

But *Newsweek* has now taken the place of the August 1987 *U.S. News & World Report* as today's least influential news weekly. And they didn't run it as a cover story, either. At long-term tops in the trillion-dollar markets, you often get a small minority opinion that is telling you to watch out. But that shouldn't stop you from using the main media thrust for your signal.

In fact, that's one way you can tell what Richard Band calls a primary top from an intermediate top. At primary tops (which usually aren't a spiked-V, blow-out top), you get some diversity of opinion. At intermediate tops or bottoms (there was an example of one in stocks during the first week of April 1994), every media outlet seems to be leaning one way.

Originally, I was going to end this book with a field trial on how I would combine the techniques of this book under actual market conditions. But now, I think that would be counterproductive. The whole point of this book is to get you to think and get away from black-box or "my-guru-told-me-to-do-it" trading.

Face it: There are no shortcuts to successful trading. You are going to have study hard and then learn (cautiously) by doing. You are going to have to look at the totality of the evidence and make those lonely trading decisions yourself. If somehow I've made that job easier for you, every minute of every hour I spent writing was worth it to me, whether this book becomes a big seller or not.

Index